Making Money
WRITING
Newsletters

From moonlighting
to full-time work, how to
set up & run a newsletter
production service

Elaine Floyd

EF
COMMUNICATIONS

Making Money Writing Newsletters: from moonlighting to full-time work, how to set up & run a newsletter production service.

© 1994 Elaine Floyd

Library of Congress Cataloging-in-Publication Data

Floyd, Elaine, 1961-
    Making money writing newsletters: from moonlighting to full-time work: how to set up and run a newsletter production service / Elaine Floyd.
       p. cm.
       Includes bibliographical references and index.
       ISBN: 0-9630222-1-0

       1. Newsletters--Publishing--Vocational guidance. 2. New business enterprises. I. Title.

Z286.N46F47   1994
070.1'75'023   93-22547

First Edition

Printed and bound in the United States of America

EF Communications   SAN: 297-4541
6614 Pernod Ave.
St. Louis, MO 63139-2149
(314) 647-6788 • (314) 647-1609 FAX
(800) 264-6305

Dedication

To my father, James K. Floyd, whose hard work, long hours and company-man loyalty unknowingly inspired me to become self-employed.

" *An entrepreneur is the kind of person who works 16 hours a day just to avoid working 8 hours a day for someone else.*"

Acknowledgements

*O*ne of the first clients to walk through my doors was a publishing man from the days of hot-metal type, Jack Whaley. Jack couldn't quite believe hand-set type could be replaced by a computer that fit atop a phone book.

I taught him about the computer and he taught me what I was *really* doing. He told me about the noise the machines used to make as the chunks of metal type would clank into place. He explained the background of terms like "leading" and "points."

Jack is now having long lunches with St. Peter. I hope he approves of the way I carry his hot-metal-type torch through my career as an electronic publisher.

Thanks also to my employees Lydia Hutchinson, Shaun Frongillo, LaJean Tietze and Jeff Runion who helped devise many of the systems presented in this book. Subcontractors Neil Harris, Les Hinton, Susan Browne and Lee Wilson taught me much about graphic design and printing arts.

Finally, I'd like to thank my husband, Alexandre Todorov, for his ever-present reminder that there's more to life than just work.

Table of Contents

List of Figures

Are you the newsletter type?

Writers: Do you write a newsletter as part of your job? Is this your *favorite* part of your job? You may be ready to start your own newsletter service.

Desktop publishers: Have you invested in your own computer? Are you an expert on using layout software to create good-looking publications? Are your friends telling you that you should design newsletters as a business? You may be ready to start your own newsletter service.

Researchers: Do you love researching? Do you thrive on sharing this information with others in a fun-to-read report? Are you a already trained as a newspaper or journal reporter? You may be ready to start your own newsletter service.

*N*ewsletters intrigue and attract. Many people find writing and designing these friendly little publications a favorite part of their jobs. They find themselves volunteering for charity newsletters or creating fun newsletters for family and friends.

If you're one of these people, consider how this love can be turned into a lucrative career or sideline. The beauty of the newsletter service is that you can moonlight, work part time or run your business full time.

Flexible structures

Some people produce newsletters in their off hours. The things you give up when leaving your full-time job (a regular paycheck and medical insurance, for instance) may inspire you to contain the enterprise to moonlighting. Moonlighting also provides an inexpensive way to test the market for your services. Ideally, you'll be forced to quit your full-time job by too much work to handle in your off hours.

For others loaded with family or other responsibilities, you may be seeking part time work. One or two good newsletter clients brings in extra income without taking all of your time.

For those developing a full time enterprise, done carefully, a newsletter service yields a good, stable income. Invest time and money wisely and take it slowly. With a handful of good newsletter clients, you'll be on your way.

To moonlighters, part-timers and full-time businesses, a world of fun and challenge awaits you.

What's inside

Newsletter services provide all or part of the talents needed to pull together a publication—including consulting, writing, design, desktop publishing, printing and mailing. This book helps you decide the specific services you want to provide and the types of customers you want to work with. This decision is reflected in your name and menu of services.

Then, the book helps you put a system in place for easing ongoing work with clients. You'll learn how to equip your office, advertise at low- or no-cost, select and keep clients, organize projects and find good vendors. Because no business is immune to change, the last chapters help you adjust to changing market conditions and find future ways to expand your business.

You're the lucky ones

Newsletter services are ideal solo enterprises that can easily grow into companies full of employees. I started my newsletter service in 1985 as a single young lass with a Macintosh Plus and a Laserwriter. By 1989, it had grown to four Macintoshes, a Laserwriter Plus, five employees and yearly sales of $250,000.

My husband to-be and I were headed for a nomadic academic life and I made the difficult decision to close up shop and hit the road with him. This lead to my writing *Marketing With Newsletters*, starting *Newsletter News & Resources* and creating a newsletter business independent of location.

Here's my best wishes to all of you lucky folks who get to live in one place, work with clients close by and write newsletters for a living.

The pen is mightier than the Ryder truck!

Elaine Floyd
St. Louis, MO (for now)

1

The market for newsletter services

$\mathcal{S}$lowly and steadily, newsletters are gaining recognition as a viable way to promote businesses, charities, associations and other organizations. Newsletters rank high in importance with brochures, flyers and ads. At some time, almost every organization considers doing a newsletter.

Desktop advertising technology also boosts newsletter recognition. The cost of typesetting and page layout has been drastically reduced. It's no accident that every page layout program lists the creation newsletters as something it makes easier.

Here's where you come in

Amongst all this hoopla, newsletters have limitations. Compared to other promotional tools, they are time-consuming, pricey, require a high level of organization and have regularly be created from scratch. These time and budgetary limitations make finding someone else (i.e. *you*) an attractive alternative to wrestling the newsletter beast in-house.

Your job in promoting your services to prospects is to zero in on these time and budgetary needs. The more ways you make creating a newsletter inexpensive and painless, the more clients you'll have. But first you must decide the types of clients you'd like to approach. This decision involves choosing the type of newsletters you want to write and design.

Categories of newsletters

Newsletters are classified as either employee (internal), promotional (external), association and church (membership), franchise or subscription. Employee newsletters help organizations keep everyone informed, trained and in good spirits. Marketing newsletters generate increased sales, donations, memberships or support. Because of their traceable effect on the bottom line, budgets are often higher for marketing newsletters than for internal ones.

Churches, associations and charities often rely on volunteer efforts to produce their newsletters. Some of the larger ones, however, have substantial budgets for outside help. Keep in mind that the philanthropic market comprises 10 percent of the U.S. Gross National Product. This is a market you should not ignore.

Franchise newsletters often start as promotional pieces for one business then are generalized to promote similar enterprises in other geographical areas. For example, a newsletter for a florist in Columbus can be modified slightly and sold to florists in Cleveland, Cincinnati and Toledo. Labor, paper and print runs are combined for a lower overall cost.

Subscription newsletters are published by those who have information others will buy. You may be in the position to start and write your own subscription newsletter. This is a tough market filled with lots of success stories but also its share of difficulties. Investigate carefully (see subscription newsletter books in the appendix). Some newsletter publishers also need desktop publishing or writing help. Your ability to get this work depends on the expertise you have.

Choosing your specialty

If you're thinking of writing newsletters, your potential clients will value your services more if you already understand the details of their businesses. You'll be in a position to suggest ideas on how to promote the business, better able to interpret industry changes and how they affect the business, and will save your clients lots of time and headaches.

The industires seeking writers with expertise are usually involve computers, law, finance and science. If you can write about software, medicine, financial markets, politics, taxes and so on, you'll find clients crying for your services. These folks also have higher advertising budgets than most retailers and restaurants.

To illustrate this point, consider that if the newsletter lands a new client for a manufacturer, it could mean hundreds of thousands of dollars and pay for the newsletter for years. If your newsletter sells a meal for a restaurant, it brings in an extra $30 to throw in the postage pot. You can quickly see why companies selling higher-ticket items will be more willing to pay the expense of a newsletter.

Perhaps you're not much for technology and finance. Lots of retailers and other independent businesses need your services, too. Often, though, you'll have to find a way to produce only one publication for several businesses. For example, you may be combining news from all of the stores in a mall or shopping district, or perhaps covering top restaurants in a certain city in one publication targeted at travel agents.

How to become an expert

What do you do if you don't already have the expertise it takes to land the higher priced jobs? Start reading.

In a few weeks of reading industry publications (regardless of the industry) you'll understand enough of any field to approach a prospective client and talk their language. And I don't mean to just bamboozle them into giving you their work.

You can place the business within the industry, position the newsletter and truly do a good job writing a newsletter that promotes the organization. Of course, you'll have to keep up with this reading to do a good job. Given an ongoing relationship, the business will gladly share back issues of their industry publications that ease your doing so.

Target markets for design-only services

Not all newsletter companies write their client's newsletters. Perhaps you're interested in design and desktop publishing only. This frees you to target a wide variety of clients.

Because every designer has a style, you may find that certain markets respond more to your work than others. Conservative organizations such as banks and law firms usually want a different look than an upscale or modern businesses like malls and travel agencies. Similar to writing services, you'll also want to find the types of organizations that have the budget to pay for your services.

Hopefully you're starting to think about the kinds of organizations you'd like to approach and the types of newsletters you'd like to write and design. Next, take a look at the possible services you can provide.

2
Developing your "menu"

You may offer clients complete production services from the initial planning to the delivery of the newsletter in the readers' hands. Or, you may research and write articles only. Perhaps you only edit. Or, maybe you exclusively do newsletter design and layout.

This chapter helps you decide the services you'll offer. Because many clients like one-stop shopping (saving time and money), you may want to team up with other people who offer the services you don't. For example, many desktop publishers work closely with writers. The designer coordinates all of the project and bills the client for both the design and writing. This way, the client sees you as offering it all. And you save the client from having to coordinate these steps.

Steps of newsletter production
First, let's look at the steps involved in newsletter creation so you'll know which parts you want to do. These are broken down into one-time set up operations, ongoing production and follow up. (See Figure 2-1.)

Newsletter set-up

Early in your newsletter career, you'll run into clients who have approached traditional advertising agencies to set up a newsletter. Then you'll discover why independent newsletter services are so competitive.

Ad agency prices of $5,000 to $15,000 are common *just for the set up.* Few businesses can afford these prices. Imagine how happy these clients will be when they hear costs in the range of $250 to $1,500 for these same services. Moreover, newsletters are your specialty so they're getting even more for their money.

Newsletter setup includes everything that will be needed before the first issue of the newsletter is started. This includes a marketing plan, a rough editorial schedule for the year, the name, the nameplate and page design and the mailing list of prospective readers (if mailed).

Because some businesses end up publishing only one newsletter, price this service separately from writing and laying out the first newsletter.

Producing each issue

You may decide to offer all or only part of the newsletter production tasks. In bidding the job, you may want to give à la carte prices and then one price for doing it all. This way, if a client doesn't have the budget for all of your services, they can choose the ones they can handle in-house and give you the rest.

Perhaps your client will research and collect information then hand it to you for final writing, editing and layout. Or perhaps they'll do a rough draft of the articles and have you polish and finish the newsletter from there (my favorite set-up). The ongoing per-issue services are research, writing, editing, proofreading, photography, custom art, clip art, page layout, print coordination and mailing services.

Additional services

Other services you can offer clients include helping them find mailing lists, keying in and storing their list for them, readership surveys and in-house training.

Figure 2-1:
Steps of newsletter creation
With slight variations, these are the steps newsletter publishers go through to create a publication.

Steps of Newsletter Creation

Newsletter set up

❏ Newsletter marketing plan
- Set objectives
- Target readers
- Outline content
- Set editorial schedule
- Decide on frequency and length

❏ Set up mailing list

❏ Give newsletter name & subtitle

❏ Design nameplate and page formats
(Includes selecting typefaces, setting up grid, etc.)

❏ Select method of distribution

Ongoing

❏ Research and write

❏ Edit

❏ Proofread

❏ Find/create photographs, artwork and graphics

❏ Typeset and layout

❏ Output final layout to laser printer or imagesetter

❏ Print

❏ Duplicate mailing list

❏ Label, sort and mail

Follow-up

❏ Mail extra issues to contributors

❏ Evaluate newsletter for future improvements

Approach mailing list storage with caution. This was the one thing that I carefully avoided. The initial set up isn't the problem. It's the onesie-twosie changes that have to be made and are handed to you on tiny scraps of paper. If you choose to offer this service, be firm on how and when updates are made, in what form the changes are given to you and your price and turnaround time. An alternative is to serve as an intermediate between your client and a mailing list storage business (see *mailing list management* and *secretarial services* in your local yellow page directory).

For some clients, you may suggest conducting a newsletter survey before they get started. For your ongoing clients, after the first year or so you may want to find out how people are responding to the publication. For both types, see chapter 6 of *Marketing With Newsletters* for more information on how to conduct statistically accurate surveys.

With many people purchasing their own computer equipment, in-house training combined with newsletter set up services may provide additional business for you. If your client is not interested in your complete services, offer the set-up/training option. This assumes that you are familiar with your client's computer and software.

Benefits of set prices & policies

The big challenge in a service industry is to clearly state what you will do and how much you will charge for it, and not be caught in a gray area where you find yourself obligated to do something for nothing.

For example, say that you give a client a flat fee to create an entire newsletter. Then, at the last minute, the client decides to cut an article. You have to scramble for a new one when you thought you were finished.

You'll be protected if you've stated in advance that your fee includes. Last minute copy changes should be addressed in your client agreement so that you can charge for the article replacement without ruffling your client's feathers or taking a beating yourself.

This way you can respond to your clients phone call with, "So you want to cut the article on page one, Joe?

Okay. But realize that it will add another $x to the price of this newsletter as listed on the price list we agreed to. Do you already have something written that I can use? Can we change the existing article in an acceptable way and save you the additional cost?"

Figure 2-2 gives details on what each newsletter task involves. The newsletter set up phase comprises mostly consulting on the project. The more you know about newsletters, the better you can help your clients during this stage.

Figures 2-3 through 2-9 are additional forms that make newsletter set-up tasks easier. Forms for ongoing newsletter production and follow-up are presented in Chapter 6.

Increasing profits with set prices

Your menu of services and related costs helps develop your confidence in your pricing. Until I had a printed price list, my face would turn crimson—courtesy of my lovely Irish blood—whenever I quoted prices.

Before you set your prices in stone, test the market. In the sample price list (Figure 2-10 on page 22), you'll notice a wide range of prices. The market in larger cities will usually bear the higher range of prices. Also, your amount of experience and the size of the company you're quoting to will directly coincide with the scale. Arriving at your set price list takes trial and error. If you get thumbs-down responses to all of your bids, lower your prices. Raise prices when you get all thumbs-up responses.

A good negotiation tactic when people want you to lower your prices, is to always get something in return—have them do more leg work, participate in the writing, reduce the size of the newsletter, pay up front and so on.

Though not always followed, strict laws on pricing do exist. The law states that you must charge the same prices to all clients. The room for negotiation comes in subtle changes to the conditions of the agreement. When working with larger operations, the project will have more levels or approval to go through and must follow stricter guidelines and so on.

Payment policies

Refer to Figure 2-11 on page 23. For first-time clients, try to collect at least a partial payment before the job goes to press. At the very least, it should be enough to cover your out-of-pocket and printing expenses.

Without being too unreasonable, try to get as much money in from your client as soon as possible. This avoids the cash problems caused by your having to pay the printer and other suppliers before you get paid by your customer. Avoid what's called *negative cash flow*—having to use your own money to pay your vendors. Many small business fail because of cash flow problems (known as *death by cash flow*). This means that on paper your business is thriving but due to clients being late in paying their bills, your checking account is in the red.

This also assumes that you negotiate good payment terms with your suppliers. Try for net 45 day terms. This assures that you'll have the time to get the money in from clients before your printing and supply bills are due. Always get postage money up front.

How does all of this sound so far? If you're interested in this line of work, your next step is to get your business operations in order.

Figure 2-2:
Description of services
Assure good client relations by clearly defining each stage of newsletter production. This protects your time when the client asks for additional work on each step. Then, it will be up to you whether or not you charge additional.

Description of Services

Newsletter set up

Establish a marketing plan

Set objectives—establish measurable goals for the newsletter. These are to be evaluated periodically.

Target readers—decide everyone who should be on the mailing list. Include clients, prospects, employees, vendors, editors of newspaper and trade journals, and other industry contacts. Maximize exposure while minimizing printing and mailing costs.

Outline content—list several ideas for content in the newsletter. Decide on several recurring features to save time and give the newsletter a structure.

Decide on frequency and length—review various lengths of newsletters. Maximize frequency to budget.

Set up mailing list—Review current list or get the list stored electronically. Consider coding names so that special issues of or inserts in the newsletter can be targeted to certain prospect segments.

Newsletter name & subtitle—Name the newsletter with something meaningful and beneficial. The name must be decided on and committed to before nameplate design can begin.

Nameplate and page design—The newsletter set-up fee includes ____ nameplate sketches and one camera-ready nameplate design. It also includes page design and sample typefaces for headlines and body copy. If none of the designs are acceptable or acceptable with changes, client will pay a kill fee equal to half of the newsletter set up charge.

Decide on method of distribution—Investigate how to mail the newsletter. Compare costs of first class, third class, piggybacking with invoices, etc.

On-going

Research and writing—Given direction and ideas by the client, research and write articles. Cut articles or last minute changes will result in a charge of $____ per hour.

Editing and proofreading—Articles are edited and proofread according to grammar and style rules set by Shrunk & White's *The Elements of Style* and the *Associated Press Stylebook* or the *Chicago Manual of Style*. The client is responsible for final proofreading.

Photographs, artwork and graphics—Created under the client's direction. In the absence of client direction, the service will use its best discretion to create the most appealing and eye-catching graphics possible. Custom-made graphics will be billed at a rate of $____ or included in a set fee. Changing of graphics will be billed at a rate of $____.

Typesetting and layout—Articles are typeset and arranged in the newsletter, placing articles in an order agreed upon by the client and service and following the design template agreed upon under the newsletter setup arrangement. Changes in the page design may result in additional charges of $____ per hour. Client must sign off on final artwork, signing for proofreading and final layout, before the newsletter goes to the printer. The client assumes liability for errors at that point.

Printing—Quality and economical printers are screened and selected. Artwork is delivered to the printer and specifications such as paper, colors, folding and quantity are given to assure best quality.

Labeling, sorting and mailing—Given mailing labels sorted in zip code order, the service will coordinate the delivery of labels, postage money and printed pieces to the mailing service. Samples will be delivered to the client as soon as possible after printing.

Follow-up

Mail extra issues—To assure good client relations and on-going relationships with others who help produce the newsletter, sample issues and thank-you notes are sent to all who contributed to the project.

Evaluation—Included with total package costs is a thorough evaluation after each issue is produced. This is completed by both the service and the client. Ideas for future issues are noted at this time along with improvements to be made in printing, mailing and so on.

Client Signature _____

Date _____

Figure 2-3:
Objectives worksheet
Written objectives help define the project and direct you in making sure it stays on target.

Figure 2-4:
(page 14)
Content worksheet
Almost every publication contains standing columns (articles on similar subjects that appear in each newsletter). Standing columns ease information collection. Generate a few ideas for these as part of the planning process.

Figure 2-5:
(page 15)
Budgeting worksheet
The businesses who produce ongoing newsletters are those who've budgeted for them. If the total cost is too much, consider shortening the publication or training the client to do more of the work in-house.

Objectives Worksheet

1. What do you want your newsletter to do for your business?

    _____
    _____
    _____
    _____

2. Who is going to read the newsletter?

    _____
    _____
    _____
    _____

3. What type of information have these customers and prospects liked to receive in the past before making a purchasing/donation decision?

    _____
    _____
    _____
    _____
    _____
    _____
    _____

4. List several ideas for articles that would provide this same information:

    _____
    _____
    _____
    _____
    _____
    _____
    _____

Content Worksheet

General areas of content	Possible feature name	To appear in each issue?
1.		
2.		
3.		
4.		
5.		
6.		
7.		
8.		

Other ideas:

Budgeting Worksheet

Option 1:   Size: # Colors: Paper: Qty: Freq.:   Other:

Option 2:   Size: # Colors: Paper: Qty: Freq.:   Other:

Option 3:   Size: # Colors: Paper: Qty: Freq.:   Other:

Description	Set-up Cost	Cost/Issue Option 1	Cost/Issue Option 2	Cost/Issue Option 3
Newsletter Design, Content, Consulting				
Research & Writing				
Editing				
Proofreading				
Typesetting & Layout				
Imagesetting/Laser Printing				
Printing				
Mailing List Set-up & Printing				
Labeling & Sorting				
Postage				

Miscellaneous Expenses
   Labels
   Art supplies
   Courier services
   Long-distance phone calls
   Fax fees
   Mileage
   Shipping charges				

Other				
Total:				
Total Cost/Year:				

Figure 2-6:
Common sizes
Clients don't necessarily have to publish four- (or more) page newsletters. Discuss the possibility of alternative formats.

Figure 2-7:
(page 18)
Name the newsletter worksheet
Some clients have already decided the newsletter's name. Others will want your ideas. Use this form for your brainstorming session. Remember to develop a subtitle, too.

Figure 2-8:
(page 19)
Available typefaces
Show clients the typefaces you have available on your system. Some companies have corporate design guidelines that direct the typefaces to be used in all promotions. If you don't have the font, build the cost of it into your quote.

Common Sizes

One- or two-page
flyer-style newsletter
8 ½ x 11"

One- or two-page
flyer-style newsletter
Legal-sized
8 ½ x 14"

(Good format for
including perforated
reply cards)

Four-page newsletter
11" x 17"

Name the Newsletter Worksheet

1. List several possible names for the newsletter:

    _____   _____
    _____   _____
    _____   _____
    _____   _____
    _____   _____
    _____   _____
    _____   _____
    _____   _____
    _____   _____
    _____   _____

2. List several ideas for subtitles (include the company name, who should read it and what benefits it provides):

    _____
    _____
    _____
    _____
    _____
    _____
    _____
    _____
    _____
    _____
    _____
    _____

Available Typefaces

This is Stone Serif

This is Stone Sans

This is American Typewriter

This is Bodoni

This is Bookman

This is Century Old Style

This is Clearface

This is Cooper Black

This is Eras

This is Eurostile

This is Franklin Gothic

This is Friz Quadrata

This is Futura

This is Galliard

This is Garamond

This is Goudy

This is Helvetica

This is Helvetica Condensed

This is Helvetica Condensed Light

This is Helvetica Condensed Black

This is Korina

This is Lubalin Graph

This is New Baskerville

This is New Century Schoolbook

This is Optima

This is Bodoni Poster

This is Palatino

This is Revue

This is Souvenir

THIS IS STENCIL

This is Tiffany

This is Times

This is University Roman

This is Zapf Chancery

Figure 2-9:
Bulk mailing form
Mailing forms provided by
the post office can help you
finalize the cost of mailing.
This one is for bulk rate
(third class) postage.

Figure 2-10:
(page 22)
Sample price list
Rates will be different
depending upon the
services. Research, writing
and design work requires
generating original ideas
and is harder hence its
higher billable rate of $40 to
$100 per hour. Errands,
data entry, straightforward
desktop publishing, mailing
and secretarial services are
"easier" and usually bill
from $15 to $40 per hour.
Prices vary greatly from city
to city and state to state.

Figure 2-11:
(page 23)
Payment policies
Negotiate the terms of
payment as part of quoting
on a job.

Bulk Mailing Form

Form 3602-R — Third-Class Regular Rate — Permit Imprint

Postage Computation — Bulk Rates

Entry Discount (If Any)	Presort/ Automation Discounts	Net Rate	Count (Pcs/Lbs)	Charge

Automation-Compatible Letter (DMM 520)

None	Saturation W/S	.124 × _____ pcs.	= $ _____
	Carrier Route	.131 × _____ pcs.	= $ _____
	5-Digit Barcoded	.146 × _____ pcs.	= $ _____
	3-Digit Barcoded	.154 × _____ pcs.	= $ _____
	3/5 Digit ZIP + 4	.161 × _____ pcs.	= $ _____
	3/5-Digit Presort	.165 × _____ pcs.	= $ _____
	Basic ZIP + 4 Barcoded	.179 × _____ pcs.	= $ _____
	Basic ZIP + 4	.189 × _____ pcs.	= $ _____
	Basic	.198 × _____ pcs.	= $ _____
BMC Entry	Saturation W/S	.112 × _____ pcs.	= $ _____
	Carrier Route	.119 × _____ pcs.	= $ _____
	5-Digit Barcoded	.134 × _____ pcs.	= $ _____
	3-Digit Barcoded	.142 × _____ pcs.	= $ _____
	3/5-Digit ZIP + 4	.149 × _____ pcs.	= $ _____
	3/5-Digit Presort	.153 × _____ pcs.	= $ _____
	Basic ZIP + 4 Barcoded	.167 × _____ pcs.	= $ _____
	Basic ZIP + 4	.177 × _____ pcs.	= $ _____
	Basic	.186 × _____ pcs.	= $ _____
SCF Entry	Saturation W/S	.107 × _____ pcs.	= $ _____
	Carrier Route	.114 × _____ pcs.	= $ _____
	5-Digit Barcoded	.129 × _____ pcs.	= $ _____
	3-Digit Barcoded	.137 × _____ pcs.	= $ _____
	3/5-Digit ZIP + 4	.144 × _____ pcs.	= $ _____
	3/5-Digit Presort	.148 × _____ pcs.	= $ _____
	Basic ZIP + 4 Barcoded	.162 × _____ pcs.	= $ _____
	Basic ZIP + 4	.172 × _____ pcs.	= $ _____
	Basic	.181 × _____ pcs.	= $ _____
DDU Entry	Saturation W/S	.102 × _____ pcs.	= $ _____
	Carrier Route	.109 × _____ pcs.	= $ _____

Total – Part A (Carry to front of form) $ _____

Check one: ☐ Automation-Compatible Flat (DMM 522) ☐ Other Nonletter – .2067 lb. (3.3067 oz.) or less

None	Saturation W/S	.127 × _____ pcs.	= $ _____
	125-pc. W/S	.137 × _____ pcs.	= $ _____
	Carrier Route	.142 × _____ pcs.	= $ _____
	3/5-Digit ZIP + 4 Barcoded*	.170 × _____ pcs.	= $ _____
	3/5-Digit Presort	.187 × _____ pcs.	= $ _____
	Basic ZIP + 4 Barcoded*	.208 × _____ pcs.	= $ _____
	Basic	.233 × _____ pcs.	= $ _____
BMC Entry	Saturation W/S	.115 × _____ pcs.	= $ _____
	125-pc. W/S	.125 × _____ pcs.	= $ _____
	Carrier Route	.130 × _____ pcs.	= $ _____
	3/5-Digit ZIP + 4 Barcoded*	.158 × _____ pcs.	= $ _____
	3/5 Digit Presort	.175 × _____ pcs.	= $ _____
	Basic ZIP + 4 Barcoded*	.196 × _____ pcs.	= $ _____
	Basic	.221 × _____ pcs.	= $ _____
SCF Entry	Saturation W/S	.110 × _____ pcs.	= $ _____
	125-pc. W/S	.120 × _____ pcs.	= $ _____
	Carrier Route	.125 × _____ pcs.	= $ _____
	3/5-Digit ZIP + 4 Barcoded*	.153 × _____ pcs.	= $ _____
	3/5-Digit Presort	.170 × _____ pcs.	= $ _____
	Basic ZIP + 4 Barcoded*	.191 × _____ pcs.	= $ _____
	Basic	.216 × _____ pcs.	= $ _____
DDU Entry	Saturation W/S	.105 × _____ pcs.	= $ _____
	125-pc. W/S	.115 × _____ pcs.	= $ _____
	Carrier Route	.120 × _____ pcs.	= $ _____

*Available only for Automation-Compatible Flats (DMM 522)

Total – Part C (Carry to front of form) $ _____

Entry Discount (If Any)	Presort/ Automation Discounts	Net Rate	Count (Pcs/Lbs)	Charge

Non-Automation-Compatible Letter .2067 lb. (3.3067 oz.) or less

None	Saturation W/S	.124 × _____ pcs.	$ _____
	Carrier Route	.131 × _____ pcs.	$ _____
	3/5-Digit Presort	.165 × _____ pcs.	$ _____
	Basic	.198 × _____ pcs.	$ _____
BMC Entry	Saturation W/S	.112 × _____ pcs.	$ _____
	Carrier Route	.119 × _____ pcs.	$ _____
	3/5-Digit Presort	.153 × _____ pcs.	$ _____
	Basic	.186 × _____ pcs.	$ _____
SCF Entry	Saturation W/S	.107 × _____ pcs.	$ _____
	Carrier Route	.114 × _____ pcs.	$ _____
	3/5-Digit Presort	.148 × _____ pcs.	$ _____
	Basic	.181 × _____ pcs.	$ _____
DDU Entry	Saturation W/S	.102 × _____ pcs.	$ _____
	Carrier Route	.109 × _____ pcs.	$ _____

Total – Part B (Carry to front of form) $ _____

Check one: ☐ Letter** ☐ Automation-Compatible Flat (DMM 522) ☐ Other Nonletter – More than .2067 lb. (3.3067 oz.) But less than 1.0 lb. (16.0 oz.)

None	Saturation W/S	.003 × _____ pcs.	$ _____
	plus	.600 × _____ lbs.	$ _____
	125-pc. W/S	.013 × _____ pcs.	$ _____
	plus	.600 × _____ lbs.	$ _____
	Carrier Route	.018 × _____ pcs.	$ _____
	plus	.600 × _____ lbs.	$ _____
	3/5-Digit ZIP + 4 Barcoded*	.046 × _____ pcs.	$ _____
	plus	.600 × _____ lbs.	$ _____
	3/5-Digit Presort	.063 × _____ pcs.	$ _____
	plus	.600 × _____ lbs.	$ _____
	Basic ZIP + 4 Barcoded*	.084 × _____ pcs.	$ _____
	plus	.600 × _____ lbs.	$ _____
	Basic	.109 × _____ pcs.	$ _____
	plus	.600 × _____ lbs.	$ _____
BMC Entry	Saturation W/S	.003 × _____ pcs.	$ _____
	plus	.542 × _____ lbs.	$ _____
	125-pc. W/S	.013 × _____ pcs.	$ _____
	plus	.542 × _____ lbs.	$ _____
	Carrier Route	.018 × _____ pcs.	$ _____
	plus	.542 × _____ lbs.	$ _____
	3/5-Digit ZIP + 4 Barcoded*	.046 × _____ pcs.	$ _____
	plus	.542 × _____ lbs.	$ _____
	3/5-Digit Presort	.063 × _____ pcs.	$ _____
	plus	.542 × _____ lbs.	$ _____
	Basic ZIP + 4 Barcoded*	.084 × _____ pcs.	$ _____
	plus	.542 × _____ lbs.	$ _____
	Basic	.109 × _____ pcs.	$ _____
	plus	.542 × _____ lbs.	$ _____
SCF Entry	Saturation W/S	.003 × _____ pcs.	$ _____
	plus	.519 × _____ lbs.	$ _____
	125-pc. W/S	.013 × _____ pcs.	$ _____
	plus	.519 × _____ lbs.	$ _____
	Carrier Route	.018 × _____ pcs.	$ _____
	plus	.519 × _____ lbs.	$ _____
	3/5-Digit ZIP + 4 Barcoded*	.046 × _____ pcs.	$ _____
	plus	.519 × _____ lbs.	$ _____
	3/5-Digit Presort	.063 × _____ pcs.	$ _____
	plus	.519 × _____ lbs.	$ _____
	Basic ZIP + Barcoded*	.084 × _____ pcs.	$ _____
	plus	.519 × _____ lbs.	$ _____
	Basic	.109 × _____ pcs.	$ _____
	plus	.519 × _____ lbs.	$ _____
DDU Entry	Saturation W/S	.003 × _____ pcs.	$ _____
	plus	.496 × _____ lbs.	$ _____
	125-pc. W/S	.013 × _____ pcs.	$ _____
	plus	.496 × _____ lbs.	$ _____
	Carrier Route	.018 × _____ pcs.	$ _____
	plus	.496 × _____ lbs.	$ _____

*Available only for Automation-Compatible Flats (DMM 522)
**Letter-size pieces cannot be claimed at the 125-piece W/S rate

Total – Part D (Carry to front of form) $ _____

*U.S. GPO: 1992-312-605/62486

Sample Price List

Newsletter set up consultation and planning $250 to $2,000
- Develop newsletter marketing plan
- Develop year-long editorial schedule
- Newsletter name
- Nameplate design
- Page template design

Research and writing	$50-$100 per hour
Editing only (agree on the stylebook used)	$50-$100 per hour
Proofreading	$25-$50 per hour
Photography	$30 to $150 per hour
Custom art	$50 to $200 per line drawing
Clip art	$5 to $20 per drawing
Page layout	$25 to $50 per hour or $50 to $200 per page
Printing coordination	$25 to $50 per hour
Mailing services	$25 to $50 per hour
Flat fee for all services	$150 to $1,000 per page

Other Services

Mailing list research	$30 to $100 per hour
Mailing list/database management	quoted per job
Readership surveys; conducting and analyzing	$25 to $100 per hour
In-house training (software, editorial skills, etc.)	$50 to $250 per hour

Desktop Publishing Services
forms, brochures, manuals, catalogs,
press releases, overheads and slides, certificates $25 to $100 per hour
($25 is typesetting; $100 is design)

Writing
press releases, catalog copy, ads, technical manuals $30 to $100 per hour

Payment Policies

Check all that apply:

- ❑ All money due before the start of the job.

- ❑ All money due before the newsletter goes to the printer.

- ❑ Partial payment before the newsletter goes to press.
  (usually 1/2 of total quote or enough to cover printing costs)

- ❑ Full payment due on delivery of printed newsletters.

- ❑ Payment due 15 days after job is completed.

- ❑ Payment due 30 days after job is completed.

- ❑ Hourly fees billed net ___ days when newsletter goes to printer.

- ❑ Printing and mailing costs billed net ____ days after newsletter is mailed.

- ❑ Postage costs due before newsletter is mailed.

- ❑ Postage costs billed along with printing and mailing fees.

- ❑ Other_____

3
Setting up shop

*O*nce you decide the services you'd like to offer, a few other things about your business need to be put into place. It needs a name, location and some initial promotional pieces.

Naming your service

When I started EF Communications, I struggled with the decision to put the word *newsletter* in my company name or not. If I included it and then wanted to branch into other forms of advertising, my name might be a drawback. This led me to my current name. My initials are *EF*, the *Communications* left my services open and the name sounded EF Huttonish—established and trustworthy.

The flip side is that for the past eight years I've specialized in newsletters under a very general name. My first year of business, a Yellow Pages editor even put me under "Communications" with the town's electronics dealers.

To keep a long story long, consider including *newsletter* in your name. The Newsletter Factory in Atlanta has a wonderful, memorable and fun name. Other ideas include: The Newsletter Group (Chicago), The Newsletter

Works (Atlanta), Newsletters Direct (Barboursville, VA), and Corporate Newsletters (St. Louis). Please note that some of these names may already have trademark or servicemark protection.

Looking back, I could have had my newsletter specialty and kept my options open with a name like Newsletters & More or Newsletters Plus.

Investment needed

There's lots of ways to finance your business. Personally, I always considered a bank loan my worst enemy. Some out there may find me a poor financial mind, but having to scrape together the money to start a business teaches you good financial habits for an ongoing operation. You also want the income you earn to go directly back into your business and not to pay interest on a bank loan.

My approach was and still is to invest time instead of money. This lets the business prove itself worthy before investing your hard-earned dollars.

How do you invest time instead of money? It involves borrowing the equipment of others (usually having to work late at night when it's idle). It may take running to Kinko's to rent their Macintoshes at 2:00 a.m. instead of sitting cozily in your office in your bunny slippers. It also means moonlighting before you quit your job—sometimes working the equivalent of two full-time positions. It may involve using older and slower computer equipment, taking more of your time to create the same layout.

Investing your own money may require cutting back on your personal expenses. One of the best books on this subject is *The Tightwad Gazette* by Amy Desczyn. You'll find that your home and business financial habits will soon take the same form. Other good ideas on funding your business are found in *Working Solo* by Terri Lonier.

Once you do have the money, you'll want to get the most from it. It's your sweat and tears after all instead of being drawn from a dusty bank vault.

Putting your money to good use

Your biggest expense will be equipping your office. This includes office furniture and supplies as well as computer equipment. When investing in computers, think carefully about whether you need to own the latest and greatest technology or if used equipment might not do the trick.

A huge inventory of used computers is now for sale. Ask at your local computer store or look in the shopping mart sections in the back of PC- and Macintosh-related magazines. You'll probably need the older versions of the systems and application software to operate it so buy carefully.

The tradeoff is that older equipment is often slower. If you're going to be doing colorful, graphics-intensive newsletters, invest in new technology. If your newsletters are mostly text with simple art pasted in at the end, older equipment and simple layout or word processing software may be all you need.

Figure 3-1 (pages 28 and 29) lists a sample of the equipment needed to run a full-service newsletter production business. It's separated into necessities and extras.

Where to draw the line on the extras

I received some great financial advice from the owner of a diaper service. He was the father of five children and had arrived to give me a diapering lesson as part of his (and my own) first delivery. I asked about all of the accessories I could buy. His advice was simple, "Use what you've got."

I've been employing that advice in areas much broader (and more fragrant).

Here are a few tips on investing in the extras. If you're going to be doing a lot of writing, a large screen monitor has its drawbacks. Its larger surface area of glare and flicker makes it fatiguing for large amounts of time spent in front of the computer. I'm writing this book on my old small monochrome monitor and switching to a 21" color monitor for the the page design and illustrations. Also note that large color monitors weigh up to 100 pounds. My Ryder-truck lifestyle doesn't care much for this.

Consider equipment that supports color carefully. Most newsletters are printed in only one or two colors. Publishing software that supports spot color, a gray scale monitor and black and white laser printer may be all you need. (The colors will show as different levels of gray.)

Equipment Necessities

Office

- ❏ Telephone with answering machine that answers the name of your business
- ❏ Dedicated work area (as simple as a kitchen table to as fancy as a full office)
- ❏ Comfortable chair
- ❏ Filing cabinet or trays and files
- ❏ Associated Press Stylebook, Chicago Manual of Style, or equivalent
- ❏ Good dictionary and thesaurus
- ❏ Computer disks for backup and transfer
- ❏ Business cards
- ❏ Coffee maker!

Computer Hardware (owned or borrowed)

- ❏ PC or Macintosh computer
- ❏ Laser printer
  (investigate printers with 600 dpi or look into upgrading an older printer)

Computer Software

- ❏ Page layout software—many word processing programs allow you to do page layout and most page layout programs can be used for word processing.

  Commonly used software:

  PageMaker, WordPerfect, QuarkXpress, Ventura Publisher, Publish It!, PFS Publisher, Microsoft Publisher, PagePlus and Microsoft Word

Equipment Extras

Office

- ❏ Copy stand (to avoid neck injuries when keying in information)
- ❏ Letterhead and envelopes
- ❏ Bright white laser paper for final printouts
- ❏ Fax machine
- ❏ Photocopier

Computer Hardware

- ❏ At least 8 MB of RAM if running Microsoft Windows or Macintosh System 7.0
- ❏ Newer PC or Macintosh with Superdrive that reads both PC and Mac disks
- ❏ Large screen color monitor
- ❏ Fax
- ❏ Modem
- ❏ Scanner
- ❏ Back up device (Syquest, Bernoulli, tape backup)
- ❏ CD-ROM drive for clip art and clip photo collections

Computer Software

- ❏ Word processing software (such as WordPerfect or Microsoft Word)
- ❏ Photo retouch software (such as Adobe Photoshop)
- ❏ Illustration software (such as Adobe Illustrator or CorelDraw)
- ❏ Clip art and clip photo collections
- ❏ Calendar making program
- ❏ Database software for your own and your client's mailing lists

I had a photocopier once and found maintaining it a real hassle. I still stopped by my neighborhood copy shop when I needed quality copies. A photocopier is probably something you can do without.

The best way to get the extras is to let client needs and projects pay for the equipment. Wait until one of your clients requires a special piece of equipment to do a certain job. Build in the cost (or at least part of it) into the price of the job. Buy only what you need, when you have the money for it. Then, you can use the same equipment for other clients. My own Superdrive, fax machine, scanner, modem and database software were paid for by client work.

Do you need a fancy office?

If you're launching a full-time enterprise and expect walk-in desktop publishing traffic for services such as resumés, your office should be accessible and presentable. However, most newsletter professionals go to their clients' offices. Some of my best clients never saw my office. I always went to theirs. For those I had to meet outside of their offices, we could have easily met at a neutral site—a restaurant, library, lobby and so on. Good office space is expensive so try doing without at first.

However, if you're the type of person who needs to get up and out of the house (if the desire to work at home just isn't there), look into sharing space with an already established business. For $100 to $200 a month, you may get someone to let you have a small room in their suite of offices. Ideally, this will be a business who may refer a client to you from time to time. Perhaps you can barter free rent for newsletter help.

What your local government needs

If you're going to be working full-time from your house, most cities require you to have a work-at-home permit in addition to your business license. If you're going to be offering full services including reselling of newsletter printing of the newsletters, you'll need a resale number that keeps you from paying taxes on the printing you buy.

Equipment Borrowing/Renting Sources

- ❑ Kinko's
- ❑ Some libraries
- ❑ College computer laboratories (some let alumni use it)
- ❑ Laptop computers
- ❑ Nice friends
- ❑ Your church
- ❑ Barter equipment use in exchange for newsletter services

Tips for Equipping an Office

- ❑ forego the decorations
- ❑ buy used desks and chairs
- ❑ buy used computer equipment
- ❑ use what you've got
- ❑ let client jobs pay for specific equipment
- ❑ barter office space in exchange for newsletter services

(You'll charge your customer the tax and submit that tax to your local government office.)

Your bureau of revenue will let you know the licenses you need. They'll check if you're in a zone where you can work from home or what additional permission or release you'll need to do so. The bureau will tell you if you must tax your service time and how to get a resale number. (This errand is not a lot of fun but is a necessary part of avoiding future troubles.)

Once you go through the steps in this chapter, you've made a good long-term investment in setting up your newsletter company. Now it's time to get revenue flowing in your direction.

4
Low-cost
& no-cost
advertising

*C*hances are that you've already begun digging around for potential clients as part of deciding if you really want to start this business. After all, clients are an essential part.

This section covers low-cost and no-cost promotional methods. It includes your own newsletter, your business card, seminars and workshops, public speaking, local publicity, writing articles, networking, a Yellow Pages listing, volunteering, your old employer and word of mouth referrals.

First, take a quick glance at Figure 4-1. It's a list of my best clients and how I found them. You'll notice that most of my clients came from *free* advertising.

Start promoting with a minimum investment of business card printing. Paid advertising is expensive and simply does not work as well as good old face-to-face selling or word-of-mouth referrals.

Your business card

Squeeze more onto your card than just your name, address and phone number. Get "newsletters" onto that card. List some of the services you offer. List a tag line: "specializing in newsletters that sell your products and services," "specializing in newsletter writing, design and production" and so on. Consider a fold-over card that functions as a mini-brochure. List the standard information on the cover and then more on your services in the inside or back side. For simple cards, consider pre-printed papers you can use to print your cards using your laser printer (see appendix). Pre-printed papers offer you the advantage of printing several versions of your card—one for newsletters, one for desktop publishing and so on.

Networking

Once you have your cards printed, it's time to get them into circulation. They do you no good sitting in that cute little box on the shelf.

Good places to network are business meetings, entrepreneurial groups, and commerce and industry-specific gatherings (accountants, architects, lawyers, engineers, etc.). You'll notice from Figure 4-1 that I had quite a few computer-related clients. This came from my own technical background that built on itself through referrals and attending industry-related meetings. These people had already seen my work and met me before I ever set foot in their offices for an initial consultation.

Let your friends know what you're doing. Friends were responsible for two good clients.

Also, let related services know about you. A desktop publishing company may not offer writing services and would be glad to team up with you on these projects. (*Note*: never take away their part of the services unless they agree. For example, don't take the publishing work yourself.) Let printers know about you. Let all area business and marketing consultants know about you. These people rely on having good services which they can refer their clients. Once you get established, offer reciprocal referrals.

Fishing from the "ex-employer" pond

My first two clients were my last two employers. This is the best reason you'll ever hear for staying on good terms with your boss. Ex-employers provide your best prospects and

Figure 4-1:
Sample client list
All of my clients were found using low-cost marketing techniques.

Sample client list

Client	Source of lead
Computer parts manufacturer	Ex-employer
Plastics manufacturer	Ex-employer
Bank	Vendor (printer) lead
Bank	Public speaking
Computer dealer	Word-of-mouth (masthead listing from computer parts dealer newsletter)
Computer dealer	Word-of-mouth (masthead listing from computer parts dealer newsletter)
Software manufacturer	Marketing consultant lead
Beauty supply manufacturer	Marketing consultant lead
Magazine publisher	Publicity in local magazine
Plastics industry association	Newsletter critique
Marine parts distributor	Business consultant lead
Outdoor/conservation group	Public speaking
Pool & spa dealer	Yellow pages listing
Laundry equipment distributor	Yellow pages listing
Restaurant/night club	Marketing consultant lead
Non-profit organization	Lead from employee
Musical equipment dealer	Our own newsletter
Industrial flooring distributor	Lead from a friend
Landscape architects	Lead from a friend
Telecommunications manufacturer	Our own newsletter (seminar attendee)
Financial planners	Newsletter critique
Industrial fuel management company	Listing in Mac User Group directory
Heating & air conditioning system designers	Business consultant lead

best word-of-mouth referrals. This assumes that you do a top-notch job while you're with them and leave their employment in the most professional, non-emotional way possible. This is hard to do *post facto*. If you're looking at leaving, start marketing now.

The benefits you offer your old employers are that you already understand their business and industry well. You know your way around the company so collecting information will be easy. The biggest obstacle will be jealousy from former co-workers who may try to trip you up—usually subconsciously but nevertheless, it's a problem. Start marketing to these people, too.

Masthead listings

Get your name in the masthead of every newsletter you do (see Figure 4-3 on page 39). The masthead is the box listing the publishers name, address and other facts about the newsletter—often confused with the term *nameplate*. Negotiate this up front when soliciting the job. A masthead listing helps spur word-of-mouth referrals (more on this in a minute).

Your own newsletter

There's no better way to convince a company you can do a good job on their newsletter than through your own publication. About now, those who know me well are going to say, "Yeah, but you were a great case of the shoemaker's children going barefoot." T'is true.

I had trouble getting my own newsletter out on a regular basis because client work always came first. Done over, I would have used what I call a "quick and easy newsletter." This is a front and back flyer or even a postcard newsletter. Then, I would have only sent it out quarterly or so, making sure that I had enough time to do client work along with my own.

To give you an idea of both types, here are two back issues of my 4-page *Newsletter News* (pages 40 through 47). Next are quick and easy newsletter formats (pages 48, 49 and 51).

Figure 4-2:
**Fold-over
business card**
Consider using a fold-over business card that works like a mini-brochure.

Fold-Over Business Card

Outside:

Corporate Newsletters & More

Linda Scoop
President
(800) 000-0000
(555) 000-0000

123 Main Street
Newstown, USA 00000

FAX: (555) 000-0001
America On-Line: 2News

Specializing in affordable:

- Newsletters
- Press Releases
- Catalogs
- Brochures

Inside:

Newsletters.

Turn your company publication into a valuable sales tool.

Providing Newsletter:
CONSULTING • TRAINING • PRODUCTION
CLIP ART • PRINTING • MAILING

Call 000-0000 for details.

Figure 4-3:
Masthead listing
Masthead listings in
your newsletters work
as small ads and
generate word-of-
mouth referrals.

Figure 4-4:
(pages 40 to 43)
**The first
Newsletter News**
This was printed on
glossy white paper in
black ink and mailed
to clients, prospects
and newsletter
seminar attendees.

Figure 4-5:
(pages 44 to 47)
**The second
Newsletter News**
This was printed on
buff-colored paper
and mailed to our
client and prospect list.

Figure 4-6:
(pages 48 and 49)
Flyer-style newsletter
A "quick & easy"
newsletter, this was
sent along with a flyer
on the books I sell.

Masthead Listing

PlastiNotes is published bi-monthly for injection molders, manufacturers and others allied to the plastics industry by Anytown Plastics, 123 Main St., Anytown, PA 00000.
To be added to the list, please call Barbara Smith at (412) 555-0000.

PUBLISHER
Anytown Plastics, Inc.

PRODUCTION
Industrial Newsletter Service
(314) 555-0000

PROOFREADING
Ben Eagle

COORDINATOR
Tress Handy

ewsletter
ews

COMMUNICATIONS

Newsletter Production Tips

Don't forget to send your newsletter to...Your suppliers – it will keep them abreast of your new product and also reinforce a "team" feeling. Plus, the salespeople of your suppliers are your best traveling word-of-mouth.
...**Non-competing, complementary companies** – these are the companies who do well when you do well. For instance, if you manufacture cameras, suppliers of film will be interested in your success. Keeping complementary companies informed is good for your business.
...**Industry press** – don't you hate it when there's a story about your industry and you're not mentioned? By sending your newsletter to the press, editors will know of your company and will have you in mind when doing special industry articles. The best compliment is when they pick up an item from your newsletter and print it in their publication (see article on Arnet).

How to stay on schedule... The best way to see that your newsletter consistently meets deadline is to borrow a technique used by magazines – the editorial schedule. Where magazines usually make year-long schedules, yours will probably be for three issues ahead. Be sure to plan for events in your industry such as trade shows, seminars, and conferences when making up your schedule. Give it a try. You'll be amazed at the time and agony you'll save.

Having "quality control" problems?...Face it, it is very difficult to proof your own writing. One method is to read the copy backwards; this forces you to look at one word at a time. An easier and more effective way is to line up some proofreaders. Someone within your company would be a good choice because of familiarity with industry names and jargon. Outside of your company, there are plenty of people who are willing to proofread in the evening. Some of the best proofreaders work as university and government assistants; they are used to reading lines and lines of copy.

Leave 'em laughing... Everyone enjoys reading the comics in the newspaper. These sydicated cartoonists brilliantly take common situations in our lives and make them seem humorous. *Doonesbury* makes fun of politicians, *Adam* and *Sally Forth* give the working woman a smile, *Tank MacNamara* is understood only by the die-hard sportsman, and kids love *Peanuts* and *Nancy*. Cartoons in your newsletter can be used to make light of your industry. These can be clipped from industry publications (be sure to write for permission) or drawn by a local cartoonist.

Producing a Newsletter When You Don't Have Time

If you conducted a survey of companies and asked them if they have ever produced a company newsletter to send to their customers,

you'd find that a good percentage have. If you then asked how often this newsletter was generated, you'd find an overwhelming number to answer, "We only produced one."

The phenomenon of the one-newsletter company has nothing to do with the success of the first issue; most say that customer feedback was favorable. It has to do with time. Either no time was available, or the newsletter was always off schedule. The Time Gremlin strikes again! The best way to keep your company out of the one-newsletter club is by using a combination of your in-house talent with an outside specialist.

In an effort to save the money, many companies assign the complete production of the newsletter to someone in-house. These people are faced with the task of juggling their agendas to fit the rigid schedule of a newsletter. Somewhere, between the daily demands of the office, time must be found to handle the entire production of a newsletter. They must not only

Continued on Page 3...

Nashville-Based High Tech Firm Has Good News

The computer industry is intensely competitive. It is characterized by aggressive entrepreneurs who fight hundreds of other start-up companies for recognition in the market. In this environment it takes a tremendous amount of momentum to pull ahead of the pack.

But Nashville-based Arnet Corporation has done it. By combining high-quality products with aggressive publicity, they have grown into a $5 million dollar company with a world-wide distribution network.

Arnet president Mike Wells credits a significant part of this success to his promotional newsletter, *The Multiuser PC News*.

Becoming Experts

From the first issue of the newsletter in November 1985, Arnet's objective has been to use the publication to position themselves as experts. "A newsletter is particularly appropriate for the market we're in," says Wells. "Because it's changing so fast, our customers desperately need summarized information on the latest computers and software."

As a result of the newsletter, says Wells, customers know that when they buy Arnet products, they're also buying industry information and expertise.

Improving Customer Relations

Another objective of the *Multiuser PC News* is to develop a personal rapport with both computer dealers and software companies. This personal contact results in the creation of an effective marketing vehicle – word-of-mouth. And it has been through word-of-mouth that Arnet has built most of its customer base.

Arnet's constantly expanding distribution network is the result of software companies and computer dealers spreading the word to other resellers. The newsletter is used to help perpetuate this phenomenon.

In order to capture the attention of dealers and software firms, each newsletter issue contains at least one profile of a computer dealer and usually a special insert on a software company. The inserts include articles covering the software company's products and employees.

One software firm had just started referring customers to Arnet when they were profiled in one of these special inserts. The company president later told Wells, "Before the newsletter came out, we wondered if we were going to get anything in return for referring all those customers to you. But the newsletter really brought a strong response."

The inserts are also used as leverage to get software companies to send copies of the newsletter to their customer lists. As a result, Arnet gets about 50 new

leads each month from this "joint marketing" effort. In addition, the company purchases mailing lists from trade associations and journals. A response card is included along with a description of Arnet's products to make it easy for potential customers to obtain information.

Not only is Arnet's newsletter used to woo customers and prospects, it's also sent to editors of industry magazines.

Complementing Aggressive PR

Arnet has come to be regarded as a source of information by computer magazine editors. In order to familiarize these professionals with Arnet, the newsletter is mailed (along with press releases) to a publicity list that contains over 900 names.

At first this may seem like a waste of paper and postage until you hear the results. During a recent press meeting, Wells was able to meet several editors because they recognized him from his picture in the newsletter.

According to Wells, knowing the editors personally directly affects the amount of coverage you are given. Arnet currently appears in top industry magazines on the average of 10 times a month. "The equivalent advertisement space would cost between 10 and $20,000 per month," he says. "Plus, editorial space is even more valuable because customers view it as more objective and credible than advertising."

Not Always Easy

Granted, Arnet's newsletter has been extremely successful, but it has also had its share of problems. Printing issues and mailing them out on time, keeping customer lists current, and following the bulk mailing process has caused many gray hairs. Also, some customers have questioned why they haven't been included in the newsletter. Several new procedures have been implemented to solve these problems. Arnet closely monitors bulk mailing and EF Communications follows strict editorial schedules which include making sure that Arnet's best customers are profiled.

Mistakes have also been made in the format of the publication. At first, it was a 16-page newsletter that included advertising. But the company felt that this publication was too long and the recipients were putting it aside in their "to be read" stack rather than reading it while going through their mail. A shorter format (without ads) was designed to be read in about 10 minutes with eye catching graphics and cartoons.

As you may be thinking by now, a newsletter can be an agonizing, time-consuming project. But busy companies such as Arnet Corporation wouldn't bother with it if it didn't produce results.

"I never could have predicted the marketing value of our company newsletter," remarks Wells. "It has become the cornerstone of our entire marketing strategy ... positioning ourselves as the leaders in our field."

Arnet Corp., Nashville, TN (615) 256-5656

Evolution of a Newsletter

Due to their frequency of publication, newsletters are more amenable to design changes than brochures and catalogs.

The following illustrate the changes made to Arnet Corporation's *Multiuser PC News* over the past year.

September 1986

January 1987

May 1987

...When You Don't Have Time

collect information and write articles but also to get the copy to a typesetter, take the type to a layout artist, and then deal with the details of printing.

But most of these editorial and production details can be economically delegated to a newsletter specialist. Your in-house writers will continue to collect information and write articles but will pass along the time consuming production and editing tasks to a newsletter consultant. The consultant takes the responsibility for the entire scheduling and production of your publication – from editorial scheduling, editing, proofreading, to the design and printing of the publication. Because this person specializes in newsletters, they know the most economical way to complete each step. Plus, their services ensure that every issue is written and produced on time.

When your newsletter is informative and timely, your customers will demand that it arrives on schedule. If it is a monthly publication, it will be expected every month. If it is a quarterly newsletter, it will be expected to be so. A prompt and consistent arrival of your newsletter on your customers' desk will reflect well on your company and will reinforce your image of being reliable and efficient. In addition, consistent repetition is important in order for you to receive the maximum feedback from your newsletter.

Frequency is just as important when sending out a newsletter as it is in placing advertising. Most experienced media buyers know

that few forms of advertising will draw the maximum "pull" on the first placement. Newsletters follow the same theory. And given the strong feedback that most companies experience on their *first* newsletter, just think of the effect you'll feel from repeat issues.

Of course, you'll have to decide how important a newsletter is to your business. If it draws a high priority, investing in an outside consultant, rather than trying to publish in-house, is often the most prudent newsletter decision you can make. From your initial conception through the final product, the responsibility is in the hands of someone else. You decide on the tone of the newsletter, chose the masthead, submit contributions, and give the final approval. That's it! Your consultant does the hands-on production of the publication.

And, by teaming up with a newsletter specialist, the Time Gremlin can't stop your newsletter from being on schedule.

Newsletter News is published quarterly and distributed free of charge by EF Communications, 1451 Elm Hill Pike, Suite 260, Nashville, TN 37210 (615) 367-1937.

To be added to the mailing list, call La Jean Tietze at EF Communications, (615) 367-1937.

PUBLISHER
EF Communications, specializing in newsletter production

EDITOR
Elaine Floyd
President, EF Communications

ASSISTANT EDITOR
La Jean Tietze

Production of your newsletter can be inexpensive and fast.

EF Communications offers any or all of the following services to assure a timely, quality production of your newsletter.

- Typesetting
  (using desktop publishing equipment)
- Editing
  (follow AP Standards used by most newspapers & magazines)
- Spell Checking
- Layout
- Masthead Design
- Photography
- Original Cartoons
- Clip Art
- Complete Coordination of Printing

Call 367-1937 or return the enclosed reply card.

Inside:

- How to get your newsletter out on time
- Newsletter production tips
- Nashville firm benefits from newsletter

Newsletter News

EF Communications
1451 Elm Hill Pike • Suite 260
Nashville, TN 37210
(615) 367-1937

![EF COMMUNICATIONS] **NEWSLETTER NEWS**

Newsletter Production Tips

Frequency and familiarity are keys to success...The effectiveness of your newsletter depends on two things: reader interest and reliability. These objectives can be achieved through frequent and regular publication using a format which fosters familiarity. Just as you look forward to standard sections in your favorite magazines and newspapers, so should your readers come to depend on standard features for pertinent news and information.

Seduce readers with graphic elements...Nothing is more forbidding than a page filled with small print. Tempt your readers to read with eye-catching graphics, pictures, diagrams, and vertical or horizontal rules. And because more isn't always better, don't be afraid of "blank" space.

A CAPITAL mistake... Resist putting headlines in capital letters. Professor Tiker of Stanford University has established that capitals actually retard reading. "Because they have no ascenders or descenders to help you recognize words," he explains, "they tend to be read individually, letter by letter."

Subheads and shorter paragraphs help readability...To help your reader digest information, it is important to break up bodies of type with subheads and short paragraphs which allow readers to pause and consider the material.

Errors can't be caught in one fell swoop...Avoid embarrassing mistakes with the four-step proofreading method. Use the first reading to get a feel for the subject and a sense of the material and the second reading to concentrate on spelling. Look for punctuation errors in the third reading, and, finally, check for over-all consistency during the fourth reading.

To check consistency ask questions such as: Does this article fit in with the others in the publication? Is everyone in the photos mentioned in the cutline? Are names spelled the same way in each mention?

One way to fill in the blank space...If your industry is prone to hot issues (ethical questions, new products, etc.) you may want to feature a question each issue. This will encourage feedback and increase readability.

Use a newsletter to expand customer base...Try sending your newsletter to mailing lists of prospective customers. Include a response card to make it easy for them to obtain information. **N**

Adding a Newsletter to Your Sales Force

by Elaine Floyd

Unfortunately, many business people overlook newsletters because they simply don't see them as sales tools. Newsletters have traditionally been either low-budget productions sent out by non-profit organizations, or specialized publications with paid-subscriptions. When taken alone, neither of these fit the image or objectives of a sales mailing piece. But when you combine their features, you get an effective marketing tool called the promotional newsletter.

Functions Like a Direct Sales Call

The best approach to producing a promotional newsletter is to imagine your salespeople calling on a customer. First, the salesperson usually discusses general happenings in your industry. Next they will talk about your new products or services.

Most likely, this will be followed up with an example of how a customer successfully took advantage of one of these products. Through this entire discussion, the salesperson has spoken (hopefully) in a tone and manner that fits your company philosophy.

The promotional newsletter follows the same format. Key elements typically include: industry news, customer testimonials, new products or services, and a profile of one of your employees. As with a good salesperson, the more informative and insightful the newsletter, the better the chance the customer will spend time with it.

Beware of Hype

Don't fall to the temptation, as many companies do, of only including news on *your*
continued on next page

Adding A Newsletter...

products or services. What you'll end up with is a product brochure and not a newsletter. Because the success of your newsletter hinges on its content, it is worth the extra time it takes to make it informative.

One way to make sure your newsletter is on target is to look at each article from your customer's perspective and answer the question, "what's in it for me?" Ideally, your newsletter will include information that makes it valuable in your customer's eyes. You may, for example, be able to include ideas that save your customers time and money.

Newsletter, Salesperson Team

Almost all industrial, high tech, and service-oriented companies use direct salespeople. Your salespeople provide customers with the information necessary to purchase your products or services. But these salespeople are limited by the number of prospects they can call on and the time they can spend with each prospect. Plus, it usually takes a few introductory calls before a prospective customer is familiar enough with your company to consider your products.

This is where the promotional newsletter can help. It can get in to see your customers when salespeople cannot and will enable hundreds of prospects to become familiar with your company at their leisure.

Elaine Floyd is president of EF Communications.

Community Service
Can Promote Your Business

by Shaun Frongillo

Businesspeople across the country have discovered that one of the benefits of publishing a promotional newsletter is the goodwill inspired by the publication. Publishing a newsletter, though, is just one form of community service.

Widespread Publicity

Here in Nashville many businesses are donating time, talent and money to help support their favorite causes.

For Kathleen Starnes of KM Starnes & Associates (an events specialist company) volunteer work is "fun" and mutually beneficial. "It's a great way to help the city of Nashville and to meet potential clients," says Starnes.

"By hooking up with well-known events, you can get a tremendous amount of very inexpensive publicity," explains Starnes. "If you're captain of a booth at the Summer Lights Festival, for instance, you can put up a sign advertising your business and expose your company's name to 500,000 people over a four-day period."

Business Help Schools

One of the more successful projects in our community is Project Pencil. This venture pairs businesses with schools to form "partnerships" in order to improve educational opportunities in Nashville. Currently, 156 local businesses have adopted a school.

According to Laurie Hughes at Edgefield Hospital, sponsor of Rose Bank Elementary School, each business brings its particular expertise and skill to the schools in an attempt to increase the quality of education at the adopted school.

Edgefield has raised money for badly needed computers and started an All A's Club.

"Everyone involved with Project Pencil is committed to education at the grassroots level," explains Hughes. "Our main objective is getting kids fired up about learning."

In a similar effort, Dalcon Computer Systems established an annual Dalcon Arts in Schools (DAIS) Award three years ago in conjunction with the Nashville Institute for the Arts. "It's designed to honor a Metro teacher deemed to have made the highest contribution to arts in education," explains Diane Diamantis, director of

---

"Publishing a newsletter is just one form of community service..."

---

marketing and communications at Dalcon.

When asked how the company has benefitted from DAIS and other projects, Diamantis replied, "Our involvement in community service projects expresses our genuine concern for Nashville and helps to associate Dalcon with something other than business."

Donations During a Cash Crunch

No matter how small your business or how limited your resources, you can play an important role in helping the Nashville community. Participation doesn't necessarily mean cash donations. Many businesses donate valuable time and services instead.

For The EAR Foundation's Balloon Classic, for example, everything from the printing of the program (donated by Harris Press) to media broadcasting (provided by WLAC) was contributed by local businesses.

To help benefit both the event and your business, make sure your achievements are publicized. One way to advertise your activities is to write about them in your company newsletter!

Shaun Frongillo is a writer at EF Communications.

EF Communications News

FAX capabilities save you money and time...EF Communications' clients can now enjoy the convenience of sending correspondence via facsimile. The machine has already saved clients hundreds of dollars in overnight mail costs and helped to keep dozens of projects on schedule. The new FAX number is (615) 399-1151.

New Macintosh drive takes PC-sized disks...Up until now, the miraculous Macintosh has had one serious drawback – PC incompatibility. After clients spent hours writing and proofing copy on a PC, EF Communications was forced to re-enter the text on the Macintosh system to be proofed yet again. But proof no more! Now, once you've finished with a document, simply save the file in ASCII format on a 5.25" floppy disk and we'll convert it to Macintosh format.

And on the subject of PC compatibility, we recently installed a Mac II which can be equipped with an add-on board to run PC-based software. So, if you have an application that requires PC compatibility, please let us know.

EF Communications helps sponsor the EAR Foundation's Balloon Classic...The company is responsible for the design, layout, and publication of the event's program. If you were unable to attend, please call for a copy of the program.

New clients...EF Communications is proud to welcome Arnet's Multiuser Systems Group, Cellular One, Dalcon Computer Systems, The Consulting Group, Goodwill Industries, Regan Controls, Applachia Service Project, K.M. Starnes & Associates, Tennessee Valley SPE, and Music Man to its client list.

Congratulations Arnet...for winning the *Nashville Business Journal's* Small Business Award in the 25-74 employee category.

New staff members offer you new possibilities...Lydia Hutchinson and Shaun Frongillo, both with advertising agency backgrounds, joined the company in January.

Lydia was formerly with Nashville-based Hart & Company. Her specialties include the production of ads, brochures, catalogs, and other print media.

Shaun, a New Mexico native, was formerly with Dye Van Mol & Associates. She specializes in writing newsletters for high-tech and industrial companies.

[Left to right]: Elaine Floyd, Shaun Frongillo, Jeff Runion, and Lydia Hutchinson.

Put Your Advertising On Hold

Karen Williams

"Please hold."... A minute goes by and you wonder if you've been disconnected. Is anyone there? Have they forgotten you're on the line? Should you hang up and call again?

Unfortunately, most businesses are forced to put their customers on hold. Fortunately, some businesses have learned that *how* you hold your customer on the line can make the difference between success and failure.

"On hold advertising is like a 'vocal newsletter'..."

According to Karen Williams, founder of On Hold Advertising, if you take care of your customers on hold, you automatically position your company as a service-oriented business.

A year and a half ago, Williams left a successful career in radio production and broadcasting to start On Hold Advertising. Her company produces casette tapes designed to take advantage of the time your customers spend on hold. The tapes combine music with soft-sell messages which advertise company services.

"On hold advertising is like a 'vocal newsletter'," suggests Williams. "It provides an added service which keeps clients informed of new products, promotions and price changes," she says.

The emphasis at On Hold Advertising is producing a soothing, professional sounding presentation. "Being put on hold is frustrating enough without being forced to listen to an abrasive ad while you're waiting," says Williams. "I put the tapes together to sound like I'd want them to if I were the one on hold."

So, next time you're held captive by the hold button, think of On Hold Advertising and what it could do for your customers.

On Hold Advertising, Nashville, TN (615) 373-1100

Do-It-Yourself Desktop Publishing...

For those of you who have your own desktop publishing equipment and want further training, there are several sources available to assist you. These are listed below and are separated by type of computer.

For the Macintosh

Training: Dalcon Desktop Systems; 321-9000. PageMaker, Quark XPress.

Users' Group: MacInteresteds; Desktop Publishing SIG meets every fourth Monday at the Peabody Campus of Vanderbilt University in the Social Religious Bldg., Room 108.

General meetings are held the first Monday of the month at Northern Telecom in Metro Center at 6:30. Call Clark Thomas at 327-1757 for more information.

For the IBM PC

Training: Computer Learning Center, (615) 244-0244. PageMaker, Ventura Publisher.

Users' Group: Music City PC Users' Group. Meets the first Tuesday of the month at 6:30 at the Belmont Business School. For more information contact Alan Ashendorf at 622-2273.

About *Newsletter News*...

Newsletter News is published quarterly and distributed free of charge by EF Communications, 1451 Elm Hill Pike, Suite 260, Nashville, TN 37210 (615) 367-1937.

EF Communications specializes in newsletter production and the desktop publishing of catalogs, manuals, and direct mail pieces.

To be added to the mailing list, call EF Communications at (615) 367-1937.

PUBLISHER
Elaine Floyd
EF Communications

EDITOR
Shaun Frongillo

DESIGN
Lydia Hutchinson

LAYOUT
Jeff Runion

NEWSLETTER NEWS

EF Communications
1451 Elm Hill Pike, Suite 260
Nashville, TN 37210
(615) 367-1937

Address Correction Requested.

Inside:

- Add a newsletter to your sales force
- Newsletter production tips
- Community involvement can benefit your company
- Customers listen to "vocal newsletter" while on hold

Elaine Floyd's

Newsletter News

Ideas & Inspiration for Promoters, Marketing Professionals, & Editors of Promotional Newsletters

Promotions, scanners & ad swaps

Scanner operators beware...

Editors and photographers are struggling over whether readers should be notified if a photograph has been retouched. (Most photos are retouched for aesthetic, not deceptive purposes.) For example, in a *National Geographic* shot, one of the great pyramids was moved in order to "balance" the frame. Associated Press has decided that the *content* of their photographs will never be changed. Manipulation is limited to standard photo methods such as cropping, dodging, etc. To avoid any feelings of deception, many publishers are using the label "photo illustration" or "photo montage" on retouched photos.

DTP 2nd most popular start-up...

The number of telephone book listings for desktop publishing services increased 66% from 2,859 to 4,734. DTP was in the top three with interesting company—baseball card dealers and massage therapists.

Swap ads for favors, goodwill...

According to *Inc.* magazine, two companies are strategically using ads in their newsletters. In California, San Luis Sourdough gives away ad space to good customers. In New Hampshire, Empire Video Superstore swaps ads in return for advertising space in area merchants' stores. The trades are effective in getting 50,000 to 100,000 pieces of promotion into potential customers' hands.

Save writing time with affordable "clip art-icles"

Tiger Communications is offering quarterly articles covering 19 different categories including business, time management, quotes, negotiation tips, and science and technology. The articles average 150 words, are copyright-free and are guaranteed to be newsworthy. Longer articles are also available. Call Rich Sheppard at Tiger Communications Group, (800) 438-4437, and ask for a brochure.

Choosing frequency, colors

The following are common questions asked during recent newsletter seminars or talks.

How often should I publish?

Repetition is crucial. The ideal frequency is between every month to quarterly. If you don't have the budget, look at ways to shorten your newsletter (see page 2). Trim a four-page newsletter to two pages. Write short news blurbs instead of long articles. While a long newsletter looks impressive on a boardroom table, it's not as likely to be read as its shorter cousin.

One color or two?

Marketing newsletters must be attractive. The first priority is to print on the best paper budget will allow. To maximize the quality of one-color designs, read *The Gray Book* immediately. If you have the extra printing budget, look at second colors that will attract attention, screen well, and appeal to your audience mix. If you're selling primarily to women, try vibrant colors like teal, fuchsia, or salmon. Most male readers (sorry, you guys aren't too exciting) prefer blues, browns, and reds.

DTP: Savior or enslaver?

Is desktop publishing all it's promised to be? Over the last six months, I've talked with many of you who are looking for easier ways to produce marketing materials.

Once you're familiar with the capabilities of your system, working with your computer is not the problem. It's the design. Choosing the placement of articles, finding the best locations for photographs, and adding the extras that make a page layout interesting take time. If you start working without a general idea of what you want, it takes even longer.

Here are a few basic tips that can free you from the mouse that binds you. First off, forego the fancy stuff. Slick is usually expensive and time consuming. Start with designs that are simple and fast to produce.

Second, train yourself on basic design principles. In the **Book News** section of this newsletter, I'll be offering reviews of hand-picked books on desktop publishing that you'll find useful. See this issue's selection, *The Gray Book*.

Make your newsletter sell for less

BEFORE: 12 pages, 60¢ each

Front.

Back page (page 12).

Lista Hank, newsletter editor for Friends of NOCCA, brought this 12-page newsletter to a Quick & Easy Newsletters seminar. The 8 1/2" x 11" newsletter was being printed twice a year at a cost of $1,200 for 2,000 copies. The organization wanted to shorten the newsletter and reach supporters more frequently while spending less time and money.

AFTER: 2 pages, 20¢ each

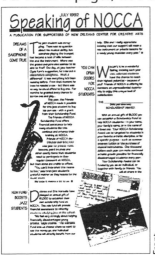

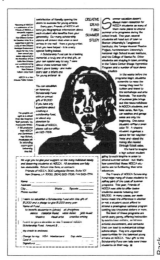

Front.

Back.

The re-designed 2-page format is faster to produce and easier for readers to skim through. The legal-sized, newsletter costs $400 for 2,000 copies including envelopes, freeing the funds to publish every other month instead of twice a year.

The "Quick & Easy Newsletters on a Shoestring Budget" seminar is available by special request from EF Communications; (800) 264-6305.

Newsletter News

Newsletter News is published by EF Communications for newsletter editors and people interested in the marketing and promotion of businesses and organizations.

Editor: Elaine Floyd

EF Communications
6614 Pernod Ave.
St. Louis, MO 63139-2149
(314) 647-6788
FAX: (314) 647-1609

Yellow Pages listing

If you spring for the big bucks and get a business telephone number (usually three to four times the cost of a residential line), you will automatically be listed in the yellow pages directory. You'll have to choose the heading you want to be under (desktop publishing, advertising, etc.). For a minimal fee, you can have a one-line description added under your name. Put something like "specializing in newsletter production" here. This additional line brought two good on-going clients. It also attracted and a handful of flaky calls, so screen prospects carefully.

Sending free critiques

Do you find yourself automatically critiquing newsletters you get in the mail? Start sending back free critiques along with information on your services. If you find typos, mention your proofreading services. If the newsletter is void of graphics, show your artistic abilities or your extensive collection of clip art. If the layout or nameplate design is dull, sketch or cut and paste their layout to show them how it could be jazzed up.

Caution here: Be kind in your critique. Chances are the editor and publisher feel pretty proud of this piece. Mention first the items that are good. Your suggestions are simply to better showcase the great job the company is already doing. You may also mention some sample prices you have for printing or mailing services. If they're substantially lower than what the client just paid, you'll have their attention and love forever.

Of course, the company can take your suggestions themselves and never use your services. Your foot is still in the door and your name is in the client's head. A strategic choice will be whether to send your critique to the newsletter editor or to the editor's boss. You want the company to pay attention to the critique but you don't want to ruffle the feathers of an editor you may end up having to work with. Use good judgement here.

Figure 4-7:
Postcard style newsletter
Done over, this is the type of newsletter I'd do bi-monthly or quarterly to promote my newsletter production service.

Figure 4-8:
(page 52)
Directory listing
Avoid paying for a large ad by adding in-column information on your business. Many Yellow Pages experts think this works better than the more expensive ads.

Figure 4-9:
(page 53)
Newsletter critique
A friend asked me to critique her newsletter. Here are my comments.

Postcard-Style Newsletter

Newsletter News

Bits and bites of news about newsletters from EF Communications 3/94
555 Main St., Anytown, US 00000   (314) 555-0000   (314) 555-0001 FAX

All caps headlines slow down readers. Use uppercase/lowercase or downstyle instead.

A spoonful of subheads helps the info go down. Help readers digest your news by breaking up articles with subheads and short paragraphs.

4-step proofing method: 1) read for overall feel; 2) concentrate on spelling and punctuation; 3) read aloud; 4) look at headlines and high-profile areas.

Reply cards repeat product line. Avoid repeating your products and services in articles. List all of them on an information request reply card.

Less can be better. Consider less type on each page and fewer pages. Encourage readers to skim your news while opening the mail.

Write like you're selling. Anyone in sales will tell you that you must interest your prospect before you can start your pitch. Imagine you're face-to-face with your reader when you're writing. Exclude anything the person wouldn't want to listen to in a conversation.

Put your newsletter on hold. Your on-hold advertising, that is. Create a tape with a friendly voice reading your company news. Callers will be treated to a vocal newsletter instead of dead silence.

FAX saves time and money. No need to call or stop by with last-minute changes. Our new fax number is (615) 555-0000.

Philanthropic reminder: tell us about your community service and donations. It's interesting news for your publication and it helps further publicize the causes you support.

Time-management tips: Enjoy on-schedule newsletter production by 1) creating and following an editorial calendar; 2) using forms and files for easy data collection; 3) subcontracting time-consuming tasts; 4) giving the project a high priority.

Local high-tech firm credits newsletter for business surge… Netnet Corp.'s one-year old publication sold over $2 million dollars worth of product last year. The once struggling firm now has a positive bank balance and expansion plans in the works.

Want to start your own business? The most popular business start-up last year was desktop publishing services.

New staff & equipment ready to take on your work. We've recently added writers and designers in addition to a full-capability pre-press facility. Give us a call for a quote on your next project. As always, our price and service can't be beat.

Desktop Publishing Service

AA Action Type
123 N. Main St.   555-1111

Alan's Secretarial Service
245 S. 2nd St.   555-1245

Corporate Newsletters Unlimited
Newsletter writing, design & printing
125 S. Anytown Pl.   555-NEWS

Bradworth's Desktop Studio
225 8th Ave.   555-3333

COMMUNICATIONS

March 15, 1994

Carol Kicker
Council on Youth & Children

Dear Carol:

Here's my initial impression of your *Spectrum* newsletter.

1. The name "Spectrum" doesn't tie in with children (or if it does, it isn't immediately obvious). Consider names like Children & Youth News, The Report Card, Kids Quarterly, The Bulletin Board, and so on.

2. The gray paper is depressing. A nice bright white would be cheerful.

3. Depending on your budget, consider printing in two ink colors. I know of a printer who can print 3800 copies of your 12-page newsletter for $1350. His one-color price is $1000.

4. The writing of the newsletter is good. It's clear and to the point and gives the newsletter a professional feel. Try using subheads to guide readers through long articles.

5. The design and layout are outdated. Consider a serifed type for body copy and a bolder type for headlines. The headlines on the pages don't stand out. For shorter articles such as the FYI section, try grouping them together under one headline (see newsbriefs sample enclosed).

6. The lines separating columns break apart continuing articles. Try using the keylines to separate different articles, not between each column.

Implement or ignore these ideas as you wish. It's only costing you a beer!

Best wishes,

Elaine Floyd

6614 Pernod Avenue • St. Louis, MO 63139-2149 • (314) 647-6788 • (314) 647-1609 Fax

Sales letters

Read your local business section, journal and magazines for leads on new customers. Ask your friends, colleagues and vendors for leads. Keep your ears open. Collect names of those you meet at business meetings. Then, mail these people a sales letter along with other information on your services.

Develop a standard sales letter that you can mail either as an introduction or as a follow-up to a telephone call. Highlight your experience, the benefits of newsletters and the advantages of giving you the project.

Seminars & workshops

Seminars and workshops include ones you develop and present yourself and those of the national companies that come through your town. Developing and presenting your own "how to do a newsletter" workshop is a great way to get clients but can be expensive. One option is to combine efforts with a printer, mailing house, your Chamber of Commerce, small business association, or business communicator group that will sponsor you and help promote the event.

Also, it's worth the $100 or so to sit in on the national workshops that come through your town (see appendix). I say "sit in" but what I really mean is to network like crazy. Put the attendance list on your computer and mail to it often. Make sure that every living soul in that room has your business card and knows the newsletter services you offer before they leave the seminar. You may even pick up a tip or two while you're waiting for the next break.

Public speaking

I landed a new client or made a strategic contact every time I spoke in public.

If you're new to public speaking—or even if you just want to have a great time—join your local Toastmasters club or speaker's association. You may even find clients here, too. If not, it's a great place to network since many of the members are professional speakers who may mention your services as part of their own presentations.

Figure 4-10:
Sample sales letter
Pack your sales letter full of information on your experience, services and benefits of newsletters. Always include a punchy opening line and a postscript (P.S.).

COMMUNICATIONS

January 3, 1994

Are you ready to try a different marketing approach for your business?

Many industrial and high-tech companies find that **newsletters provide customers with the information needed to purchase technical products**. In addition, when you send your customers and prospects a newsletter, they perceive your company as a leader in its field.

If you have been frustrated by trying to explain your products to non-technical advertising agencies, you'll be relieved to know that **EF Communications specializes in producing technical materials**. My background in chemical engineering has proven vital for understanding and writing about industrial products.

In addition to newsletters, we also produce brochures, catalogs, manuals and forms. Because we use the latest technology in desktop publishing, you benefit from faster turnaround times and lower prices than traditional typesetting.

If you're ready to get a fast start on 1994, please call or return the enclosed reply card.

Best wishes for a booming '94,

Elaine Floyd
EF Communications

P.S.   Please pass along the newsletter to anyone else involved in your company's marketing.

6614 Pernod Avenue • St. Louis, MO 63139-2149 • (314) 647-6788 • (314) 647-1609 Fax

Opportunities for other speaking engagements are local business groups, writing and design meetings, computer user groups and any other organization you can think of whose members would be interested in newsletters.

Keep your focus of finding new clients in mind. Don't charge a speakers fee, research and develop your presentation carefully, target it to the particular audience and give oodles of free advice. The more you give, the more your audience assumes you know. And the more you tell them how to do a newsletter, the more they'll want you to do it.

Often, especially for larger organizations, the fact that you're local may be a drawback. Some groups prefer out-of-towners (as the old saying goes, an expert is someone who comes from at least 100 miles away).

Publicity

Having your services mentioned in an article in your local paper is the best advertising that money could buy. But money can't buy it—only your savvy and good luck can.

Figures 4-11 and 4-12 show articles that served as incredible booms to my business. Both of these were initiated by me by submitting a sample piece on how to write a promotional newsletter.

If you do your own newsletter, make sure your local newspapers and radio stations are on your list. This may spur them to report on your business, too.

Articles for local or national publications

This is one promotional tip that I never used myself though others have and successfully. The idea is to show your expertise and establish credibility within your local market by writing as a guest columnist for a national magazine or publication. The true value of these (and of publicity, too) are the reprints you get of the article. Include them in your information package that you give to every new prospective client.

To have your article published, you need to write a query letter outlining your idea to the magazine editor.

Figure 4-11:
Business magazine publicity
This article appeared two months after I opened my company. Through it I found a typesetting client that was with me for the duration of my service.

TECHNOLOGY

Office Equipment Market Update

by Peter Jordan

Desk-Top Publishing: Everyone's a Publisher These Days

When Franklin publisher Bill Smith bought the trade magazines *Southern Lumberman* and *Furniture Production* recently, he contracted with a typesetter for his first issues. A hefty typesetting tab left him thinking about alternatives.

"Desperation was the mother of invention," quips Smith, who also publishes Nashville's *Key Magazine*. He sank $8,000 into a personal computer system, became his own typesetter, and joined the desk-top publishing revolution — perhaps the most explosive development in personal computing since spreadsheets.

The essence of desk-top publishing is the ability to format and edit text into columns first on a screen, then on a page, and also to create multiple font styles and sizes. Beyond that basic capability, many programs include the ability to integrate graphics with text. High resolution display is an important feature of some systems, and the ability to manipulate multi-page documents in an integrated fashion is also impor-

tant. Finally, many programs feature sophisticated hyphenation routines and several automatically eliminate pesky widows — a last line of a paragraph which carries over to the top of the next page or column.

Time and Money

Fueling the demand for desk-top systems is a basic business consideration: saving time and money.

Elaine Floyd, owner of EF Communications here, which publishes four newsletters plus resumes, brochures and special projects, enthusiastically agrees: "With my business, desk-top publishing helps control costs, typographical mistakes, and turnaround time by eliminating the typesetting step. A four-page newsletter can be taken from concept to print in a matter of three days." Floyd uses a Macintosh, Pagemaker software and an Apple Laser-Writer printer.

Above: Elaine Floyd with the Macintosh Pagemaker that produces her newsletters and brochures.

"I can write it, edit it and lay it out all in one sitting, rather than write it, take it to the typesetter, approve the layout, and then have to deal with typographical errors and other changes. If the customer wants a change, I can just sit down and change it."

The result is text closely mimicking a typesetter's work.

Though Floyd still uses a conventional typesetter for the final version of some brochures, she says that newsletters lend themselves extremely well to desk-top publishing. "You don't need quite the clarity of real typesetting, yet it still looks professional," she notes.

For the projects that do need conventional typesetting, Floyd writes it and lays it out with her Mac, then takes the disk to her typesetter, who has a Macintosh that interfaces with a Linotype system. An increasing number of desk-top publishing systems are able to drive typesetters directly, eliminating the need to rekey documents, a clear time and money saver.

Beyond Newsletters

The potential uses of desk-top publishing systems go far beyond newsletters and magazines. Anything a business puts onto paper can be enhanced by the typesetting and layout features of a personal publishing system driving a laser printer.

"One specific application where the Macintosh really shines is in designing forms," asserts Floyd. "Laying out and updating previously designed forms is much simpler and less costly. Different line weights can be drawn, boxes can be screened in, and you always get a straight line, no matter how unsteady your hand.

"It's also great for sample layouts," she continues. "If I had a full-blown ad agency, I don't see how I could get along without this. With a Mac I could do mockups in a few minutes."

Editors don't like to receive the full article if you've submitted the same one to competing magazines.

For more information on writing query letters and for ideas of where to send them, see *The Writer's Marketplace* published by Writers Digest. It's available at most bookstores. Also, look in your library for *Standard Rates & Data* directories on all of the magazines published in the U.S.

Working for free or reduced prices

When you're just starting out and need some filler of sample newsletters for your portfolio, consider working for free or drastically reduced prices for strategic clients. For example, I gave bargain rates on a newsletter for a marketing consultant. In exchange, he passed along my name to his clients who needed newsletters.

When working for reduced prices, make sure your client knows that you've lowered your prices for them. The last thing you want passed along is that you offer cheap rates.

Car signs

If you are constantly in your car running errands for clients, have a sign made for your car. Realtors have these kinds of signs. Temporary signs are nice because they can be removed for your own privacy or security.

Volunteering

In the newsletter seminars I've taught, almost half of the newsletter editors also volunteered their expertise to a cause they supported.

It's a beautiful gesture to help a cause you love with your talents. When you're just getting your business off of the ground, though, you may help a charitable organization for more selfish reasons. Like working for reduced prices, carefully choose volunteer projects for maximum or strategic exposure to the clients you're after. That doesn't mean you only help big charities. Your 250-copy neighborhood association newsletter may be more willing to give you a small ad and put you in touch with better prospects.

Figure 4-12:
Business journal publicity
Right after I moved to a larger office and hired two additional people, this business journal article appeared. It brought much needed exposure and clients.

Business Journal Publicity

Publishing newsletters far cry from engineering for small firm's president

By Matthew Brayton

Like many successful people who stumbled into their career niche, Elaine Floyd didn't exactly envision running her own small company specializing in the production of newsletters while attending the University of Louisville.

The Santa Paula, Calif., native majored in chemical engineering while at the school, but says she realized during an internship at the DuPont plant in Old Hickory that the "regimented lifestyle" of an engineer wasn't her style.

After graduating in 1984, Floyd signed on with Washington Pen Plastic of Pittsburgh as a Nashville-based sales representative for the southeastern United States, a job that called for a lot of traveling throughout Alabama, Arkansas, Kentucky and Mississippi.

It was that experience that first got her interested in promotional newsletters.

"I just wanted to give a consistent message to everybody ... and usually you didn't get to say what you wanted to tell them anyway," says the president of EF Communications.

So she began using newsletters not only as a "great way not to travel so much, but also as a way of calling on people."

When the newsletter she was printing solely for her region became a big hit with Washington Pen Plastic executives, she decided to develop a promotional newsletter for the entire company, which the firm had typeset and printed professionally.

And when she saw how much was paid to have the production work completed, she made another decision — to personally finance a MacIntosh printer and microcomputer with the $500 the executives had planned to spend monthly to develop the newsletter.

She used the equipment for the company and also picked up work with Arnet Corp. in Nashville, helping the computer hardware company's sales staff with a newsletter of its own — a move she says helped "turn around" the then-struggling company.

Floyd eventually had three newsletter contracts when she founded EF Communications, and now has 10 with a "few in negotiations," she says.

Two weeks ago she moved her office down the hall to a larger office in the building where she is a tenant on Elm Hill Pike. She already has an assistant working for her full-time, and says she will add a part-time worker soon, she says.

Floyd says the development of desktop publishing technology is doing a great deal in allowing small- and medium-sized companies to expand their customer-base.

Moreover, she says the smaller companies — often hidden in the shadows of industry giants — are now able to make their images "look a little bigger in the whole sea of things."

Since June 1986, Floyd's small consultation and production company has been helping other smaller organizations

Elaine Floyd, EF Communications   Photo by Bill Thorup

get the word out on themselves to competitive markets through the use of promotional newsletters.

And some companies with sales staffs of less than 10 — especially those that sell technical products — are finding the newsletters to be extremely thorough and cost effective.

"At a time when the average sales call costs $229, imagine having a representative that can make one for less than $2 — and this 'employee' doesn't need a company car or an expense account," Floyd says.

Companies with only a few people dedicated to the field or to telephone sales can add leverage to their sales calls and effectively extend the sales force, Floyd says.

Her promotional newsletters "are a combination of the 'folksie'-style of information found in a church newsletter and the 'inside' information found in a subscription newsletter," she says.

"It includes profiles of a company's employees and customers along with in-

dustry news, all conveyed in a personal tone. When done correctly, it functions as a means of maintaining existing customers along with attracting new ones."

Newsletters produced by smaller companies can be effective when they aren't overdone like many promotional brochures developed by large companies, she says.

Floyd says all newsletters are produced for the reader, be it for a company, an idea or product. People produce newsletters to help communicate in large groups and convey information that otherwise would slip through the crack of a typical sales call.

"If you're trying to fill the bathtub, that is, fill your customer base, you want to make sure while pouring water into the bathtub, none of it escapes down the drain," Floyd says.

"Newsletters are essentially the plug in the bottom of the tub. People use newsletters to communicate with customers, and thus to maintain the customer base." ■

Just because this isn't paid client work, treat it as if it were. This is vital to the best promotional tool on the planet—word-of-mouth referrals.

Word-of-mouth referrals

Assure good word-of-mouth referrals by being what's called the *consummate professional*. Take your clients' best interests to heart by saving them time and money whenever possible. Become an expert on your subject matter, on writing well and on current designs. Meet all deadlines or let the client know the minute it looks like things are off schedule. Establish and communicate your pricing, services and methods of operation up front. Remind your client of these when necessary. And never lose your cool. In other words, aim to be the best, and then be a bit better than that.

Of course, all your best efforts mean nothing if falling on deaf ears. Next, let's look at how to hook up with clients that treat you the same way and respect the efforts you're making.

Figure 4-13:
Sample car sign
Advertise on the road with a magnetized car door sign.

5

Finding good clients

*y*ou may find it a bit overly optimistic to read about "selecting" your clients thinking you'd be glad to have whatever business comes along. But there are lots of potential clients out there waiting for your services. Your job is to attract, screen, grab and keep these clients.

Screening clients

Life is too short to spend your time working around people that you don't enjoy. It's much, ***much*** too short to work around those who don't make you feel good about your work. All of us stick with these situations from time to time just to make ends meet. But once you have other options, *get-out-a-there.*

There's more newsletter work than all of us can handle. Your challenge is finding clients you enjoy, who have the money to pay you and who will continue to fund and support a newsletter project.

No matter how much interest a client shows in you, look carefully at the company's stability. Concentrate on the long term; your profitability depends on it. The clients who publish newsletters quarter after quarter, year after year are the ones who "keep the bulldog fed."

Approach new companies and those in financial troubles with caution. The benefit of helping out struggling businesses are that their doors are not being beaten down by your competition and they'll greatly appreciate your help.

Impressions of success can be deceiving. One of the richest, most successful businesspeople I know carries a Bic pen and a steno pad (no Mont Blanc and leather day planner). Don't be so impressed with a teakwood conference room that you don't check credit references. (You can buy a Dun & Bradstreet credit report for $60—see appendix.)

Follow the client screening checklist in Figure 5-1. The answer to most of these questions should be "yes" before you continue. If you get the feeling the client is looking for a fast boost to business, suggest more aggressive methods such as direct selling, telemarketing or flyers for a great sale or deal. A newsletter is a *long-term* promotional tool. They usually don't get as quick of a response as price-slashing sales do.

Selecting flexible clients

Once your docket fills up, you may be select clients based on their flexibility. Most newsletters are either monthly, bi-monthly or quarterly. Twice a year—in January and July—you'll be producing newsletters for everyone at the same time. It's hectic.

Steady your work load by finding clients who will publish off the traditional schedules. We found bi-monthly newsletter business for December, February, and so on. A few quarterlies were willing to come out February, May, August and November instead of January, April, July and October. Keep this in mind once your newsletter machine gets cranking.

For moonlighters, you'll be looking for companies willing to meet during lunchtime or after hours. Finding neighbors who need newsletter help is a great way to get started. These clients bring work home and you stop by and pick it up. (Volunteering for your neighborhood association newsletter is not a bad idea for finding business owners or managers in your neck of the woods.)

Figure 5-1:
Client screening checklist
This list helps you determine the long-term potential of a prospective client.

Client Screening Checklist

Client Name: _____

Contact: _____

Phone #: _____

Date: _____

Does the client have:

- ❏ enough information to put into a newsletter issue after issue.

- ❏ the necessary funds to dedicate to several issues.

- ❏ the support of its top management (if applicable).

- ❏ a product or service priced high enough that extra sales will pay for the newsletter.

- ❏ a product or industry that changes fast enough that customers rely on a newsletter to keep them informed.

- ❏ other planned promotions that the newsletter can support or be worked into.

- ❏ a rapport with you that makes for a profitable and fun working relationship.

- ❏ the view of a newsletter as a long-term marketing tool (not a last-ditch effort to get them out of serious trouble).

Selling your service

We've come to the point of that all-so-important first meeting. Here you are to present your ideas for the client's newsletter in hopes that they will find you charming and bright enough to want to give your their business.

I still remember the knot I'd get in my stomach as I parked my car to go into those first meetings. A quick glance in the mirror would confirm that the Cream-of-Wheat was off of my face. Over to the passenger seat found business cards and a pen. Portfolio? Check. Charm? Check.

You approach the receptionist with the I've-done-this-a-thousand-times-before bluff. Lower the voice and say, "Newsletter queen (king) here to see Ms. X and Mr. Y."

Enter the meeting, say "no" to the coffee (it's too easy to have a mishap while spreading out your wonderful newsletters) and then shut up.

What? Be quiet?

Yes. Your job now is that of a reporter. Ask as many questions as possible about this company. What other marketing, employee, membership and donor communications are they doing? What do they expect the newsletter to do for them? How often will they publish, which parts have they decided to do and what is their budget? Do they have some sample newsletters that they want to model theirs after? Has this project been approved or does some higher-up still need convincing?

Once you find this out, *then* you can talk about your services, your experience and your ideas for working the newsletter into their current marketing plan. Pull out some similar newsletters you've done or collected. Show how you can help. This allows you to target your presentation to the needs of your client.

A vital part of your presentation is to give your client ideas on ways to reduce costs by using your services. There's probably some initial cost estimates already in the manilla folder that's sitting right there on the conference table. Suggest design tips that require printing in two colors instead of three. Bring along the low-cost papers that your printer stocks. Discuss publishing a smaller piece more

Figure 5-2:
Sales presentation checklist
As you're packing your briefcase before your first meeting, take a quick inventory of what you'll need.

Sales Presentation Checklist

- ❏ business cards

- ❏ pen and paper

- ❏ sample newsletters

- ❏ copies of publicity you've received

- ❏ portfolio

- ❏ service menu or company brochure

- ❏ a list of typefaces you have on your computer

- ❏ referral letters

frequently that the 12-page gazette they're thinking of. Show sorting and mailing methods to reduce postage costs.

While you don't want to divulge all (names of lower-priced vendors you've ferreted out, for example) you do want to show the client that you are a conscientious service dedicated to providing not the cheapest price, but the greatest value for their money. This includes quality of information, design, paper, printing and mailing services. (Nothing looks worse that a beautifully printed piece with the mailing label smacked on at an obtuse angle and covered by postal machinery gunk.)

Don't worry if your ideas are the same as the client already has; you've proven that you're on their side.

Quoting on the job

While at this meeting, you may be quoting fees on the spot or you may be collecting information for submitting a formal quote. Your set price list will give prospects a ballpark figure. Then, with the information you collect at the meeting, you can submit a formal proposal along with printing prices in a few days. This gives you time to collect printing costs, sketch out a few rough ideas and digest what you learned in the meeting.

Once you submit your quote, the client will either accept or reject it. If it's rejected based on price, investigate other ways you can work together. Don't undersell your services. For every reduction in price you take, make sure that the client is either doing more of the leg work, reducing the size of the job, and so on.

If all of your proposals are accepted, consider raising your prices a bit—just to the point where you lose a job now and then based on price.

Client agreements

Before we get started on this, let me say that I'm not one for air-tight legal agreements. In order to have an agreement that protects you in armour, you end up with a stack of paper that treats your potential client as the enemy, not the apple of your eye.

Figure 5-3:
Quotation form.
Along with your quotation you may want to include the description of services shown in Figure 2-2.

your name & address here

Quotation

Contact:_____

Company:_____

Address:_____

_____

Phone #:_____

Quotation #: _____

Page ____ of ____

☐ Revision of an earlier quotation
    (#_____)

Date: _____
Quotation good for 30 days.

Project Name:_____

Services Description	Est. Time	Rate/Hr.	Flat Fee	Total

Printing Description	Paper	Size	# Colors	Quantity	Total

Mailing Description	Rate	Quantity	Total

Postage	Cost/Piece	Quantity	Total

Miscellaneous		Total
Imagesetter paper or film/Laser prints		
Phone calls/Faxes		
Courier service/Shipping/Mileage		
Supplies		
Taxes		
Other		

Notes: **Estimated Total for Job:**_____

That said, some sort of client agreement is good to establish up front what you will and will not provide. This aids in good client relations by avoiding any mis-communications. People tend to read things they have to sign more carefully.

If you do need something that will stand up in court, find a good, relaxed lawyer that understands the importance of client relations.

Some newsletter services require clients to commit to a set number of issues. The willingness of a client to sign a year-long contract tells you something about their budget and seriousness. This helps you find the profitable year-after-year kind of business that keeps you going. The resistance you may find is that this is a big commitment for someone who has never worked with you. An alternative is to have a trial issue then go to a yearly contract. Charge more for the trial issue than for subsequent ones.

A committed contract also helps your client save money. It gives you the room to negotiate for lower yearly fees from mail houses, printers and other vendors.

Keeping your clients

So you've found a good client, finished a few newsletters and you newlyweds are happily strolling along. How do you make the honeymoon last?

The way to any client's heart is through top notch service. It's the extras that count. Never, ever let yourself say, "oh, that's good enough." Take the extra few moments to make a layout perfect, a sentence better. Make suggestions on improving each issue. Use the evaluation form shown in Figure 6-8.

One of extras you can do is conduct a readership survey. You may want to offer this for free to clients who've been with you awhile. A survey will be a good addition to your portfolio, improve the newsletter and help your client's customer relations.

You also provide extras by expanding your talents. Keep up with the newsletter industry through magazines, professional groups, seminars and newsletters. Fresh ideas are part of what clients pay for. If you don't have them,

Figure 5-4:
Sample contract
Please note that this example is for your general knowledge only. Read through it to get a general idea of what can go wrong. It was not drawn up by a lawyer and may not protect you legally. Please use it as a general guideline, as a way to communicate with your client or as an outline to take to a lawyer.

Client Contract

This agreement is being made on the _____ day of _____, 19____ between _____ ("Newsletter Service"), and _____ ("Client").

1. Work Ordered

Client is contracting Newsletter Service to provide the following goods and services:

_____ .

2. Payment and Terms

Client agrees to pay Newsletter Service the following:

a. Flat fee of _____ .

b. Hourly fees. Client agrees to pay Newsletter Service $_____ per hour plus out of pocket expenses. Time fees will be billed for time spent in completing the project described above, including: telephone conferencing, art layout, writing, _____, _____, and time spent on required traveling. Out of pocket expenses to be reimbursed include: postage, travel and lodging expenses, long distance phone calls, messenger services, _____, _____ and _____ .

c. Terms

Payment are be:

_____

Claims for defects, damages or shorages must be made by the customer in writing within a period of 30 days after delivery. Newsletter Service's liability shall be limited to stated cost of any defective goods. Past due accounts bear interest at the rate of 1.5% per month.

3. Rights Granted

a. Exclusive license—Newsletter Service hereby grants an exclusive license to Client for use of the material created for the project or as follows:

_____

b. Non-exclusive license—Newsletter Service hereby grants a non-exclusive license to client for use of the materials created for the project or as follows:

_____

Any and all intellectual property rights created by Newsletter Service and/or its subcontractors shall be the sole and exclusive property of Newsletter Service. Upon breach and/or termination of this contract by Client, any and/or all rights licensed to Client hereunder shall immediately revert to Newsletter Service.

4. Disclaimer of Warranties

Newsletter Service hereby disclaims any and all implied warranties of merchantability and/or warranties of fitness for particular purpose. In no event shall Newsletter Service be liable for any person and or entities consequential and/or incidental damages. Any and/or all damages shall not exceed the funds actually received hereunder by Newsletter Service.

5. Indemnity Agreement

Client further agrees to indemnify and hold harmless Newsletter Service for claims of any nature whatsoever pertaining to the services and goods provided. This includes loss of customer furnished proofs and materials, missing projected deadlines set for the completion of work, and loss of any information stored in Newsletter Service's computers. Additionally, this Indemnity Agreement includes claims relating to any software or other copyrightable materials furnished by customer, and from any and all copyright claims and/or misappropriation of trade secrets and/or any claim of theft of proprietary information.

6. Quotation

A quotation not accepted within 30 days is subject to review.

7. Orders

Orders regularly entered, verbal or written, cannot be cancelled except upon terms that compensate against loss.

8. Experimental & Preparatory Work

Experimental and preparatory work performed at customer's request, such as sketches, drawings, composition, plates, presswork and materials will be charged for at current rates and may not be used without the consent of Newsletter Service. Artwork, type, plates, negatives, positives and other items when supplied shall remain Newsletter Service's exclusive property unless otherwise agreed in writing.

9. Revisions

Revisions represent work performed in addition to the original specifications. Such additional work shall be charged at current rates and be supported with documentation upon request.

10. Proofs

Corrections are to be made on "master set" and returned marked "O.K." or "O.K. with corrections" and signed by customer. If revised proofs are desired, request must be made when proofs are returned. Newsletter Service regrets any errors that may occur through production undetected, but cannot be held responsible for errors if the work is printer per customer's O.K. or if changes are communicated verbally. Newsletter Service shall not be responsible for errors if the customers has not ordered or has refused to accept proofs or has failed to return proofs with indication of changes or has instructed Newsletter Service to proceed without submission of proofs.

11. Overruns or Underruns

Overruns or underruns not to exceed 10% on quantities ordered up to 1,000 copies and/or the percentage agreed upon over or under quantities ordered above 1,000 copies shall constitute acceptable delivery. Newsletter Service will bill for actual quantity delivered within this tolerance. If customer requires guaranteed "no less than" deliver, percentage tolerance of overage must be doubled.

12. Delivery & Freight Fees

Customer is liable for any and all shipping, transportation and handling fees incurred in the production of his order. Materials delivered from customer or his suppliers are verified with delivery ticket as to carton, packages or items shown only. The accuracy of quantities indicated on such tickets cannot be verified and Newsletter Service cannot accept liability for storage based on supplier's tickets. Title for finished work shall pass to the customer upon delivery, to carrier at shipping point or upon mailing of invoices for finished work, whichever occurs first.

13. Force Major

Newsletter Service shall not incur any liability or penalty for delays due to state of war, riot, civil disorder, fire, strikes, accidents, actions of Government of civil authority and acts of God or other causes beyond the control of customer or Newsletter Service.

14. Third Party Shipping

In the event any material necessary for the production of customer order must be shipped to a third for additional processing, binding, color separation, typesetting, photographic work, or press work, Newsletter Service will incur no liability for losses incurred in transit or due to the delay of the shipper of the third party.

15. Choice of Law

The customer and Newsletter Service hereby intend for the laws of the state of _____ to govern the validity and performance of this contract. Sole and exclusive venue for any and/or all claims and/or courses of action between the parties shall be in _____ County.

Client: _____

Date _____

Newsletter Service _____

Date _____

some other newsletter pro may take away your client. Continue to search for ways to save your clients money (see Figure 5-5).

If you're operating a single-person office, it's often tough to keep your current customers happy while trying to find new work. When faced with a time management decision, always give your current client the priority. Their newsletter may not be as exciting or challenging as a fresh project, but it's putting food in the bulldog's dish.

One last item that's important to customer relations is to watch your p's and q's. This means understanding copyright law and other legalities of publishing. For example, what if your client gives you a cartoon for the newsletter that's clipped out of the Sunday paper? You know you'll be violating copyright law and need to get permission. You may do this as part of your services or provide a form for the client to do it. But you must remind the client of the risk they take by not getting permission.

For professional services, follow the compliance guidelines set by their trade associations. Lawyers, financial planners and others have strict rules for advertising. Include the boilerplate disclaimers in their publications.

Taking care of problems quickly

The biggest potential you have for problems is in meeting critical deadlines (such as having newsletters in time for a trade show), typographical or other types of errors in the layout, sloppy printing and low-quality mail services (labels on sideways, not on time, lost newsletters).

First, try to avoid these problems. Use the time management techniques set up in Chapter 6. Choose vendors according to Chapter 7. Hire a good proofreader and build this into the cost of your services. Have clients sign off on final artwork. Never take changes to final layouts over the phone; always get the client to put them in writing. (If you must take verbal changes, carefully document them.)

When a problem does arise, start by working directly with the vendor. Negotiate a re-print of the job or lower fee. With newsletters usually containing timely information, re-running the job may not be an option. But if it is and the

Figure 5-5:
Ways to save money
Here are a few ideas on how you can help your clients' newsletter budgets.

Ways to Save Money

- ❏ Encourage and train your clients to do as much of the writing and research as possible. Trade magazines and industry information comes across their desks or phone lines every day. With a bit of training from you, they can learn to turn this into valuable newsletter content.

- ❏ Discourage frequent design changes. Spend the time at the beginning to come up with a format and stick to it.

- ❏ Learn all you can about using screens and page layout software so that a one or two color publication is all you need.

- ❏ Encourage clients to stick with standard-sized newsletters.

- ❏ Collect all of the costs involved in producing the newsletter. Look for ways to keep each individual cost under control.

- ❏ Buy a year's worth of paper.

- ❏ Negotiating yearly printing contracts.

- ❏ If staff is available, suggest that the client does their mailing in-house. Give them contacts and information about how to get a bulk rate permit number.

- ❏ Change the paper to a less expensive stock. This doesn't necessarily mean giving up on quality. Through smart shopping (working with your printer) you can find equal or better quality stock for less cost.

- ❏ Streamline the time management of this project.

problem was the printer's fault, don't hesitate to insist that the printer re-run the job. This happens often and is part of everyday printing life.

The most common problem directly attributable to you may be the variance from a quoted price to the final price. Do your best to realistically quote on a job and hold to your quote. If your customer changes the job specifications after you've started work, it is your responsibility to revise your quote as soon as possible. Perhaps printing numbers are changed, a page added and so on. If you're charging by the hour and the time the job is taking goes over the allotted amount, you must talk to your client and reach an agreement. Let your client know when you're nearing the allotted time. This is the moment to inform your client, not right before you make the final invoice.

Meet problems head-on and as quickly as possible. Saying you're sorry is a critical first step. The second step is being more concerned about the problem than your customer is. Keep your client informed about every step you're taking.

Statistics show that clients are more loyal to suppliers that have quickly solved a problem to their satisfaction than to those suppliers that they've *never* had a problem with.

Consider any problem a potential marketing opportunity. Do your best to solve it quickly and put procedures in place that assure it never happens to your customer again—even if it means taking money out of your profits to do so.

Extra work from clients

It takes much less advertising to get additional work from your existing clients than to find new clients. Once you're familiar with your client's operations, helping create other marketing and promotional pieces is a natural for you. For example, if you're writing up new products and services, new employees, awards won, etc., the same items, with some alteration, can be used in press releases, flyers and information for the company's catalog.

You're in an ideal spot to provide publicity services. Your experience as a newsletter editor helps you speak the

Figure 5-6:
Copyright assignment
Again, this is not an airtight legal agreement since laws vary greatly from state to state. Use a form like this when seeking permission to reprint an article, cartoon, photograph or other work.

Copyright Assignment

Name of publication:_____

Please complete and return promptly to:

> *your name & address here*

Name:_____

Address:_____

I am licensing to Newsletter Service and/or its clients:

❑ One-Time Use: I hereby grant North American Rights for one-time use (the copying, distributing, displaying, performing, and derivating) of the work(s) in the above -listed publication for:

_____

❑ First-Time Use: I hereby grant First North American Rights for one-time use (the copying, distributing, displaying, performing, and derivating) of the work(s) in the above -listed publication for: _____ I warrant that the work(s) are previously unpublished.

❑ Exclusive License: I hereby grant the exclusive right(s) to use the work(s) for:

_____

❑ Non-Exclusive: I hereby grant non-exclusive license to copy, distribute, display publicly, perform publicly, and derivate the work(s) for: _____

I warrant that the material submitted is an original work of authorship authored and owned solely by myself and does not violate any other person or entity's copyright, trademark, rights of publicity, right of privacy, and/or any other such right.

I agree that any submitted material is subject to editing and that publication cannot be guaranteed. I acknowledge the ownership of copyright rights in any edited version belongs to Newsletter Service as original creations of derivative works. If I sell the submitted material for use in any other magazine or other medium, I acknowledge that I do not have the right to use the edited version. Further, I am licensing nonexclusive rights for the use of the produced work(s), at no additional compensation, in any Newsletter Service promotional material/profudct and further licensing the copying and distribution of reprints of the work(s).

Title of work(s): _____ Payment: _____

Executed this ____ day of _____, 19 ____

_____   _____
Author/Artist Signature   Newsletter Service

language of magazine and newspaper writers. You know that they don't want to hear a bunch of hype. They want straightforward, interesting news. They don't want to be bothered and won't make a commitment on when the piece will run. They appreciate those who help them meet their deadlines and provide quality artwork, facts, survey information and so on.

Make sure the client is aware the ensuing savings in time and money. The artwork and photographs you collect for a newsletter article can be used in the press kits, brochure or catalog. Once you're onsite for an editorial meeting, you can pick up the rough draft of a form the personnel department needs typeset. It's easier for your client to only have one vendor coming through the door than several.

That said, you don't want all of your eggs in one basket. Try to spread out your clients without any taking more than 33 percent of your time. For most small services, this is tough to do. One big cheese usually provides over 50 percent of your revenue. That's okay. Just make sure you start a "rainy day" savings account that will keep your bulldog fed for three months or so if you are ever to lose your largest client.

A key way to assure you have the time to pick up additional work and not depend on one big cheese is to practice streamlined time management. The next chapter shows you how to run a tight ship.

6
Organizing for maximum productivity

*Y*ou can let one or two clients take all of your time. You'll run to and fro, scramble to meet deadlines and generally get on everyone's nerves.

Or you can spend the same amount of time, have 10 clients, bill five times as much and run a well-oiled newsletter production machine. I think I know which one you'll choose.

Managing the time gremlin

The time gremlin is a tough beast to tame. Harnessing it requires that you organize not only yourself but also your clients and possibly even your vendors. This involves putting in place planning and procedure (eeeek!).

First, you must make your clients see that the biggest cost of producing a newsletter isn't printing or postage, it's time. You need their support in keeping your own time to a minimum to save them on fees. This same structure also saves *their* time and assures timely completion of each project. You'll have to strike a balance here. If most clients knew up front how much of their time a newsletter takes, they may not want to do one.

Setting up an editorial board

Time management requires setting up and conducting regular editorial board meetings. During these meetings, you plan the content for several issues in advance (see Figure 6-1). You split up the tasks involved in doing each issue and place these tasks into a realistic schedule (see Figure 6-2, page 80). Then, everyone sticks to the schedule.

(For some clients, placing the information in Figure 6-2 into calendar form works well. We used a program on the Macintosh called Calendar Maker. Several PC and Mac calendar programs are available.)

Sounds a bit formal for a simple newsletter, doesn't it? But having a set group to make decisions about the newsletter content is important. If working with a larger organization, you'll need to coordinate with several different people. These people need deadlines and need to know that you can't be expected to jump through hoops if they don't keep up with the schedule. Of course, you're the vendor so you must be soft in your demands but at the same time firm. It's in the best interests of your client that you're sticking to a set schedule.

When working with smaller clients, the editorial board may consist of just you and the client. Still follow the format of having a set meeting every issue and create a schedule for you both to follow.

The following forms also help clarify a newsletter project into the parts you'll be doing, when they'll be done and what will be involved. If you're to juggle several newsletter projects at once, your clients must understand that their failure to meet a deadline could mean a delay in the project.

Systematized content collection

In between each newsletter project, ideas and materials for the newsletter will come your way. Set up files separating information for the newsletter—newsbriefs, customer focuses, new products, future ideas and so on. Give your clients reporter forms (see Figure 6-3, page 81) they can fill out immediately after a noteworthy event has occurred. You can easily use this information to write up a good story.

Figure 6-1:
Editorial schedule
An editorial schedule gets the pain of planning out of the way for the year. It guides you from issue to issue and frees your clients from making these decisions each issue.

Figure 6-2:
(page 80)
Project flow sheet
Give all people involved in the newsletter project (you, your client, your vendors) a copy of the project schedule

Figure 6-3:
(page 81)
Reporter form
Copy and distribute this form to all people involved in collecting information. A good group of reporters makes for easy compilation of information. A form like this makes it easy for non-writers to help with newsletter articles.

Editorial Schedule

Client: _____

Newsletter: _____

Issue Date	Feature:	Feature:	Feature:	Feature:	Notes:

Project Schedule

Client: _____

Newsletter: _____

Task	Assigned To	Time Needed	Begin Date	Proof Date	Final Deadline
Finalize Content					
Approval from Client					
Collect Information					
Write Articles					
Find/Create Graphics					
Edit Articles					
Approval from Client					
Layout					
Proofread					
Camera-Ready Output					
Approval from Client					
Print					
Run Mailing Labels					
Mail/Distribute					
Follow-up					
Other:					

Reporter Form

Client:_____

Newsletter:_____

Reporter Name:_____

Phone #:_____

Story Idea or Title:_____

_____

Who is involved/invited: _____

_____

_____

What is the event: _____

_____

_____

When did it (will it) happen: _____

_____

_____

Where: _____

_____

_____

Why did it (will it) happen: _____

_____

_____

How did it happen: _____

_____

_____

Other details: _____

_____

_____

Other people to contact: _____

_____

_____

You'll find that for other types of information collection, such as interviewing, that you ask the same questions and follow the same pattern each time. Develop set questionnaires to use for different types of interviews (see Figure 6-4).

Once the layout is complete, both you and your client will proofread it carefully. Though all agreements state that the client is responsible for final proofing, errors still reflect poorly on you. Use the proofreading guidelines shown in Figure 6-5 and give a copy to your client with the proof. Make a stamp similar to that shown in Figure 6-6 to imprint on the back of all final artwork. The client must sign this before you send the job to the printer.

Follow-up forms

During the creation of each newsletter, you'll have various people involved with the newsletter ask for additional copies after it's printed. Make note of these requests on a newsletter follow-up form that you keep with the project. Then, when the newsletter is off press, pull out the form and use it to send out requested copies. A form like the one in Figure 6-7 keeps you from digging frantically through your notes for a lost address. You'll also use this form to remind yourself to permanently file a copy of the newsletter in your portfolio and send a newsletter evaluation form to the client.

It's a good idea that both you and your client complete an evaluation form after each newsletter project while future ideas are fresh in your minds (see Figure 6-8). Follow up on all suggestions and put a copy in the client's file. Consider using 2-part NCR forms so the client can save a copy, too.

Internal organization

One of my biggest fears when doing client work was that I would lose a photograph, article or another original piece of art. That fear led to a rigorous organizational method using job envelopes.

I'm happy to report that we never lost a thing. Over the years, the job envelopes' utility expanded to include more

Figure 6-4:
Interview form
Each newsletter will probably have its own version of this form.

Figure 6-5:
(page 84)
Proofreading checklist
Use this as a guideline for your internal proofreading and that of your clients.

Figure 6-6:
(page 85)
Proofreading stamps
Stamp all final artwork with these proofreading and approval stamps. Have clients sign off on artwork before it goes to press.

Interview Form

Reporter Name:_____

Story Idea or Title:_____

Possible Angle:_____

Spelling of name: _____

Title: _____

Company name:_____

Phone/Fax number:_____

Address: _____

□ Must approve article (get fax number)

Would you like additional copies of the newsletter? How many?:_____

Is a photo available (request it to be sent immediately):_____

Why is this person important to readers?_____

_____

What is their history with your company?_____

_____

What product/service do you provide this person?_____

_____

What does the customer/employee like best about your company?_____

_____

How has the interviewee benefitted from working with/buying from your company?

_____

_____

_____

Additional questions:

_____

_____

Additional questions:

_____

_____

Other sources to contact: _____

Proofreading Checklist

Client: _____

Newsletter: _____

Text:

- ❏ Read everything once-through for overall feel
- ❏ Read through for punctuation and spelling
- ❏ Read all articles and headlines aloud
- ❏ Look at headlines only
- ❏ Read headlines and most visible text backwards
- ❏ Check spelling of all names and company names
- ❏ Call phone numbers to verify
- ❏ Confirm date of newsletter
- ❏ Confirm date of copyright
- ❏ Other:
- ❏ Other:
- ❏ Other:

Layout:

- ❏ Artwork straight
- ❏ Typefaces correct
- ❏ Bulk rate indicia included (if used)
- ❏ Consistent spacing between elements (headline & body copy, column width, etc.)
- ❏ Phone number and contact information included where needed
- ❏ Other:
- ❏ Other:
- ❏ Other:

Printer's Proofs/Bluelines:

- ❏ No specks or unusual marks
- ❏ Photographs in correct place
- ❏ Correct crop and screen on photos
- ❏ Color break correct (if printing in more than one color)
- ❏ Other:
- ❏ Other:
- ❏ Other:

Proofreading & Approval Stamps

PROOFED BY:

_____ DATE _____

_____ DATE _____

REVISIONS:

_____ DATE _____

_____ DATE _____

FINAL APPROVAL:

CLIENT _____ DATE _____

EFC _____ DATE _____

than just holding bits and pieces of information. They were the center of the operation.

Job envelopes (shown in Figure 6-9, page 89) record all information about the specifications, printing and billing of the job. This is written on the outside of the envelope for easy access. The job name is written both on the top of the horizontal and vertical sides to make it visible when in an elevated file tray or sideways in a slatted stand. The contact name and phone number are also included. Some clients may require purchase order numbers for billing. For those clients, get the number before your start on the work and record it on the envelope.

Copies of all other forms are stored in the job envelope. The original quote, notes from meetings, quotes from printers, purchase orders and more are all kept together. At first, we stapled the job envelope forms to 9x12 manilla envelopes. Later, we had them printed directly on white envelopes.

Once you're busy with lots of clients, consider using job numbers on the envelopes for traffic management (see Figure 6-10, page 91). Also list all expenses, printers quotes and fees necessary to cut the final invoice. This will be an incredible time saver.

These envelopes have an additional time-saving of avoiding the hunt for that one scrap of paper you need to finish a job. (Newsletter projects involve lots of small pieces.)

How to use the job envelopes

When we received the go ahead on a job, we assigned a job number to the project. Required purchase order numbers were listed on the job at this time. The quote form was added to the envelope. So was the nameplate design and any other preliminary sketches.

The envelope was stored in a central area of the office. This way, it was accessible to the writer as she worked on the copy. Then, the desktop publisher could find it when all of the material was ready. Once the job went to the printer, it was turned over to the office manager for invoicing.

Figure 6-7:
Follow-up form
Assure professional follow-up of each newsletter with the following form.

Figure 6-8:
(page 88)
Evaluation form
After each newsletter comes off the press, give your client and yourself one of these forms to complete. Fill in the upper section of the form and mail it to your client.

Figure 6-9:
(page 89)
Job envelope
Here's the core of your internal paper-taming machine. Enlarge this form by 130% and staple it or print it on 9x12 envelopes.

Follow-up Form

Client:_____

Newsletter:_____

Date/Vol. #:_____

❑ Sent copies of newsletter with thank-you notes to contributors

❑ Filed copy of newsletter in permanent portfolio file

❑ Sent client evaluation form

❑ Other:

❑ Other:

Notes:

Contributor's names & addresses:

Name: _____ ❑ # of copies: _____

Company:_____

Address:_____

City/State/Zip:_____

Name: _____ ❑ # of copies: _____

Company: _____

Address: _____

City/State/Zip:_____

Name: _____ ❑ # of copies: _____

Company: _____

Address: _____

City/State/Zip: _____

Name: _____ ❑ # of copies: _____

Company:_____

Address:_____

City/State/Zip:_____

Name: _____ ❑ # of copies: _____

Company:_____

Address:_____

City/State/Zip:_____

Evaluation Form

Client: _____   Date: _____

Contact: _____

Newsletter: _____

Date/Vol.: _____

(Please return a copy of your newsletter with corrections marked in red along with a copy of this form.)

What general changes or additions would you like to see in the next issue?

_____

_____

_____

Please use this section to comment on specific changes:

Printing:
- ❏ Paper _____
- ❏ Ink colors _____
- ❏ Overall quality _____
- ❏ Turnaround time _____
- ❏ Other _____

Design:
- ❏ Layout _____
- ❏ Nameplate _____
- ❏ Typeface _____
- ❏ Photographs _____
- ❏ Illustrations _____
- ❏ Other _____

Editorial:
- ❏ Length of articles _____
- ❏ Number of articles _____
- ❏ Writing style _____
- ❏ Typographical errors _____
- ❏ Turnaround time _____
- ❏ Articles or suggestions for next issue: _____

_____

_____

If you have additional comments or suggestions, please call.
WE LOOK FORWARD TO MAKING YOUR NEXT NEWSLETTER EVEN BETTER.

Job Envelope

Client, Job Name: _____

Job Name: _____

Company: _____
Address: _____
City/State/Zip: _____
Contact Name: _____
Phone #: _____ FAX #: _____
Directions to this location:

Job #: _____
P.O. #: _____
Invoice # _____
Invoice # _____
☐ Bill time & printing separately.
Deposits/Payments
Date   Amount
_____

Date	**Service** Time Description		Hrs./Mins.	Rate/Hr.	Total

Amount Quoted: ___ ☐ Call before quote is exceeded   Total Service: ___   Profit Margin: ___

Date	**Expense** Description	Miles	Cost	Tax	Total:

Date	**Printing** Description	Quantity	Cost	Tax	Total

Amount Quoted: ___ Amount Paid: ___   Total Printing: ___   Profit Margin: ___

Date	**Mailing** Description		Quantity	Rate	Total

Amount Quoted: ___ Amount Paid: ___   Total Mailing: ___   Profit Margin: ___

Date	**Postage** Description		Quantity	Rate	Total

Total Invoice: ___   Total Profit Margin: ___

Notes:

Invoice often, invoice quickly

For cash flow purposes, consider billing jobs in two separate invoices—one for the writing and layout and one for the printing and mailing. Because a two-week delay is between when you finished a job and when the newsletter is printed and mailed, you want the invoice for your time to be well on its way to being paid. You start your time investment at least two weeks before the job is finished. You don't want to have a whole month go by before you can cut an invoice (and then wait another month before it's paid).

Another useful form for tracking incidental expenses is a long distance telephone log that you keep by your phone. If you're doing long interviews and so on, you'll need to be reimbursed for this (see Figure 6-12).

Personal time management

Time comprises the majority of the profit on your invoices. It's your product when running a service business. Use it and guard it like a family heirloom.

I'm a recent day planner convert. Like any recent convert, I'm a bit evangelical but here's my story anyway.

After seeing several friends use these little books to juggle work, home and squeeze a bit of fun to boot, I was convinced to investigate. (I chose the Franklin Day Planner because it builds professional and personal tasks together.) My investment was $100. It has easily paid for itself in one month. The day after I set up my planner, I removed from my office:

- ❏ my rotary card file
- ❏ a bulletin board
- ❏ 4 items taped to my wall
- ❏ 3 items on Post-It notes stuck to my computer
- ❏ a separate calendar used for speaking engagements
- ❏ a "to-do" notepad
- ❏ a desk pad/calendar
- ❏ 3 home shopping lists stuck to my refrigerator
- ❏ 2 other lists stuck in my purse

I transferred my project planning for the coming year to the project worksheets in the planner and then organized them

Figure 6-10:
Job number log
Once you have a handfull of clients, start assigning job numbers.

Figure 6-11:
(page 92)
Quote number log
Use this log to track the quotations made using the form in Figure 5-3, page 69.

Figure 6-12:
(page 93)
Invoice
This will soon be your favorite form of all.

Job Number Log

Date	Job #	Client	Job Name	Date Due	Date Closed

Quotation Number Log

Date	Quote #	Client	Job Name	Revision?	Receive Job?

your name & address here

Invoice

Invoice #: _____

Contact: _____

Purchase Order #: _____

Company: _____

Terms:

Address: _____

Date Due:

_____

A monthly charge of 1.5% of the invoice amount will be charged to all overdue accounts.

Phone #: _____

Project Name: _____

Services	Time	Rate/Hr.	Flat Fee	Total

Printing	Paper	Size	# Colors	Quantity	Total

Mailing	Rate	Quantity	Total

Postage	Cost/piece	Quantity	Total

Miscellaneous	Total
Imagesetting or laser prints	
Phone calls/faxes	
Courier service/shipping/mileage	
Supplies	
Taxes	
Other	

Total Due: _____

by priority. Then I backed out individual tasks onto the monthly planning lists. In one short month, this planner has saved me time and money. It's helped me project into the future, avoid last-minute delays and allowed me to use couriers and bundle errands together for maximum productivity. I also have all of the information on my business I need when I'm away from my office.

Boss in a book

For self-employed, solo workers a day planner functions as your boss. It keeps you focused on the long-term and helps you organize the tasks that efficiently lead to the completion of projects.

Invest in some type of day planner, set up long-term projects on the project schedules and carry this book wherever you go. Your clients will be impressed by your level of organization, you can realistically schedule projects and avoid running around feeling like your always behind.

You'll soon see the difference in your profitability, your reliability and in respect from your colleagues and co-workers.

Now that you have yourself and your clients organized, you need to get your vendors in line, too.

Figure 6-13:
Invoice number log
Keep close track of your accounts receivable using this log. Start calling for payment the minute you sense trouble. The squeeky wheel gets the check.

Figure 6-14:
(page 96)
Long-distance log
Long-distance telephone costs add up quickly. Assure reimbursement by logging your calls.

Invoice Number Log

Date	Invoice #	Client	Date Due	Date Paid	Notes

Long-Distance Log

Date	Job #	Phone #	Purpose	Est. Time	Amount

7

Finding good & cost-effective vendors

*I*f you're to provide one-stop newsletter shopping, you'll need some good vendors in your corner. You'll want price-effective, quality and conscientious folks who stick to your schedule. You may need artists, writers, desktop publishers, imagesetters, photographers, printers, mail houses and list management companies.

Weeding out the duds

My husband laughs every time he sees me writing about how to choose vendors. His amusement stems from the troubles I've had along the way with my own.

I've had some vendors who were simply fantastic. They provided good quality work, top-notch service and were a joy to work with. Other times, I wasn't so lucky. I've had vendors who treated my schedules like works of fiction, produced sloppy work and created errors that embarrassed me with my clients. I obviously didn't think this would happen when I chose the vendor.

Because the vendors you work with are such an important part of your overall image, take the time put each one through the test in Figure 7-1. Surprises can still happen but a bit of careful scrutiny takes little time and screens out the majority of potential vendor duds. (By the way, I'm having much better luck after putting it into place.)

Price is still a factor

Most advertising agencies and newsletter services build in an upcharge (or handling charge) of 15 percent of printing and other subcontracted services. If you're to provide better pricing than your clients can find themselves, you either need to work with vendors who will give you a discount or find those who only work with wholesalers.

Word of mouth referrals help you find good vendors. Some wholesalers such as printers are located in back warehouses or basements. They may or may not be listed in the Yellow Pages.

I found my favorite wholesale printer through a forms company. He worked alone in a rundown area of town in a small shop. His business has since grown to six people and he now works in a warehouse section. His prices are still half of what I'd pay elsewhere and his quality is top-notch. His turnaround time is a bit longer than a commercial printer, though.

My backup printer was a commercial house that could provide more fancy jobs. I negotiated lower prices with this printer. She knew that I always stuck to schedule and provided complete artwork ready to go on press. This saved the company time and helped them plan their work load.

Finding a good mail service is also tricky. Most of the mail houses listed in the Yellow Pages are set up for mailings larger than a 3,000 piece newsletter mailing. You'll be lucky to even get them to call you back. Look for smaller shops. Newer vendors will need your business more and may even give you lower prices if you're willing to bring in mailings during their more slack periods.

The final artwork for some newsletters goes straight from a laser printer to press. Others use the higher resolution output of a Linotronic imagesetter. Many printers now offer these services though, your basement wholesale printer may not. Printers who offer imagesetting usually offer it at more competitive prices than service bureaus.

Figure 7-1:
Vendor dud checklist
Put your vendors through the paces before you hand over the precious work of your clients.

Vendor Dud Checklist

❑ Question low prices. Find out how the vendor is set up to do this. See samples of their work. A low price may mean lower quality. Find out if this is acceptable. Some vendors just starting out in the market may be offering more competitve rates. This is a good opportunity for you to get good work while helping a fellow entrepreneur.

❑ At the same time, find out how long the vendor has been in businesses. Weed out fly-by-nights. Make sure a new vendor is committed to the new business.

❑ Find vendors who are set up for and want the kind of work you have.

❑ Don't give someone work just because you like the person. Liking your representative has nothing to do with the quality of the work. Make sure the representative is involved in your job. Make sure that your rep not only sells you but also has a hand in quality control and production. Look for a rep who spends a good bit of time looking over job production.

❑ Take plant tours whenever possible. Pick up random samples of the work they're creating. (Remember that samples in the portfolio are their best jobs.) Look for organization and cleanliness.

❑ Give small test projects. Gradually work into your involvement with the vendor as they prove themselves. Don't rely on a new vendor for a time- and quality-critical project.

❑ Do press checks. Let the printer know you'll be there for the press run. Do the same with your mail service. I learned this from a friend's father who always insists to be present when a mechanic works on his car. He's had no problem with shoddy workmanship since he started this practice. (By the way, he knows nothing about cars.)

❑ Remember that your client sees your vendors as a reflection of *you*. Find vendors who have your same quality and service standards and work style.

❑ Ask about realistic turnaround times. Make sure this fits with your needs.

Also check the imagesetting services listed in the back of computer magazines. Some will turn the job around in less time using express delivery and still save you money. Try a trial run before you get an out-of-town service involved in a project for your best customer.

Assure good communication whenever you send jobs to printers, imagesetters and mail houses using the forms shown in Figures 7-2, 7-3 and 7-4.

Clarifying copyright ownership

When you subcontract services such as photography, artwork or writing from another person, you need to clarify in writing exactly the rights you're buying (Figure 7-5 on page 105). In the absence of a written agreement, you are buying a one-time usage right. This means that you or the client can't use the same photograph, art or article in a company brochure, press kit and so on without the permission of the artist or author.

One-time usage is usually all you actually use but it's tough to keep track of. Do your clients a favor and negotiate the right to use art, photos and articles custom made for the job as you please. The ideal is to negotiate complete rights but non-exclusive rights will do.

Maintaining good vendor relations

Keep your vendors interested in your projects and following your schedules. While you want to negotiate good payment terms (hopefully net 45) always respect these terms by paying on time.

Learn as much as you can about your vendor's business. Go through a complete plant tour. Learn about the vendor's equipment and capabilities. Involve vendors on how to save your client money and speed up turnaround. This assures that you and your vendor work together as efficiently as possible. It also helps you refer other business to your vendors.

Let your vendors know when you're looking for additional clients. The more work you give a vendor, the more interconnected your businesses become. Involve your vendors in the marketing you do. If you produce your own promotional newsletter, ask for a break in the print

Figure 7-2:
Print purchase agreement

Figure 7-3:
(page 102)
Imagesetting purchase agreement

Figure 7-4:
(page 103)
Mail house purchase agreement
Avoid potential problems caused by unclear communication by putting all job specifications in writing.

Print Purchase Agreement

your name & address here

Job #: _____

Representative: _____

Printer: _____

Address: _____

_____

Phone #: _____

Date Due: _____

Please note that failure to notify us of any delays 3 days prior to this due date will void this agreement.

Payment Terms: _____

Project Name: _____

❑ Mock-up included

❑ Confirmed price: _____

❑ Quantity*: _____   *This the minimum needed; underruns are not allowed and overruns not billable.

❑ Size: ❑ 8 ½ x 11   ❑ 8 ½ x 14   ❑ 11x17

❑ # Pages: ❑ front only   ❑ front & back   ❑ 4-page   ❑ ____ pages

❑ Fold   fold____times down to _____(dimensions)

❑ Perforations: as marked on mark up copy

❑ Paper: ❑ weight: ___   ❑ name:_____   ❑ color:_____   ❑ finish:_____

❑ Ink Color: ❑ black   ❑ PMS # _____   ❑ PMS#_____   ❑ other: _____

❑ Photos: ❑ scanned in   ❑ need____halftones

❑ Screens: ❑ on artwork   ❑ need_____ cut

❑ Artwork: ❑ camera-ready

❑ copy on disk, printer to typeset & layout

❑ layout on disk; printer to imageset

❑ Blue line or other proof required

❑ Press check required: Call_____ at _____when ready for press

❑ Packaging required: ❑ in boxes ready to ship   ❑ shrinkwrapped in   s

❑ Shipping: ❑ customer pick up   ❑ deliver to mailhouse at:

❑ deliver   samples to client at:

❑ deliver   samples to address above

❑ deliver balance to address above

❑ Ship via:

❑ Special instructions:

Imagesetting Purchase Agreement

your name & address here

Representative: _____

Service bureau: _____

Address: _____

_____

Phone #: _____

Job #: _____

Date Due: _____

Please note that failure to notify us of any delays 1 day prior to this due date will void this agreement.

Payment Terms: _____

Contact: _____

Project Name: _____

❑ Storage medium: ❑ PC disk 3.5"   ❑ PC disk 5.25"   ❑ Mac disk

❑ Program used: _____ Version: _____

❑ Saved as EPS or other: _____

❑ File name(s): _____

❑ Mock-up included

❑ Typefaces used: _____

_____

❑ Linked artwork/files included on disk and noted on mock-up

❑ Confirmed price: _____

❑ Page size: ❑ 8 ½ x 11   ❑ 8 ½ x 14   ❑ 11x17   ❑ Custom: _____

❑ # Pages: _____

❑ Output: ❑ paper   ❑ resin coated (RC) paper   ❑ film

❑ Separations: ❑ 1-color   ❑ 2-color   ❑ 3-color   ❑ 4-color   ❑ other: _____

❑ Resolution: ❑ 600 dpi   ❑ 1200 dpi   ❑ 2,400 dpi   ❑ other: _____

❑ Line screen: ❑ 85   ❑ 110   ❑ 133   ❑ other: _____

❑ Delivery: ❑ call for pickup   ❑ send by courier
              ❑ ship via _____ to: _____

❑ Special instructions: _____

Mail House Purchase Agreement

your name & address here

Representative: _____

Mail House: _____

Address: _____

_____

Phone #: _____

Job #: _____

Date Due: _____

***Please note that failure to notify us of
any delays 2 days prior to this due date
will void this agreement.***

Payment Terms: _____

Project Name: _____

❏ Mock-up included

❏ Confirmed price: _____

❏ Quantity: _____

❏ Postage deposit of $_____ received by ____ (initials)

❏ Labels: ❏ peel & stick   ❏ cheshire   ❏ to be output

❏ Zero-waste mailing (all names must be mailed)

❏ Fold: fold _____ times down to _____ (dimensions)

❏ Inspection of mailing required before shipped; call _____

❏ Remainders: ❏ customer pick up   ❏ deliver to us
               ❏ ship to: _____
               _____

❏ Special instructions:

pricing. After all, if you get more business, they get more business.

You and your vendors each have stakes to make sure that the other remains profitable in a variety of economic conditions. This brings us to the next chapter—adjusting to business fluctuations.

Figure 7-5:
Works for hire agreement
In the absence of an agreement like this, you only have one-time rights to any of the work your subcontractor's create.

Works For Hire Agreement

your name & address here

Artist/Writer: _____

Address: _____

_____

Phone #: _____

Publication Name: _____

I hereby assign to the company listed above ("Newsletter Service")and/or its clients any and all copyright and/or other intellectual property rights I may have in the material listed below and submitted to Newsletter Service.

To the extent permitted by United States Copyright laws, the work submitted is a work for hire. In the event that this work is not a work for hire, any and all copyright rights are assigned to Newsletter Service.

I warrant that the work(s) assigned are unpublished, original works of authorship authored and owned solely by myself and does not violate any other person or entity's copyright, trademark, rights of publicity, right of privacy, and/or any other such right.

Title of Work (s): _____

Payment:

Date: _____

Artist's/Writer's signature:

_____

8
Adjusting to business fluctuations

*A*s a small operation, you'll surf the tide of the boom and bust times. It's easy to ignore potential business downturns when you're on the rise. Though I encourage you to enjoy the good times, do a bit of preventative maintenance for harder times, too. Here are some ideas for adjusting your service to the good and the bad (but not the ugly).

First, the not-so-good

A year after I moved my business from Nashville, the once strong area economy went into a slump. Several of my former clients fell on hard times. They either canceled their newsletters or moved them in-house.

At the time, I was resettling in New Orleans and working on shifting my operations to book and newsletter publishing. Amid these distractions, I stopped and projected what I would be faced with if I still had a newsletter service in Nashville. Layoffs? Perhaps having to close my office and work at home for awhile? Would I have gone completely out of business?

I'll never know the answers to these questions but I

can tell you what I *probably* would have done.

My desktop publisher was moving away. I wouldn't have replaced him with anyone. Then, I would have:

❑ Cut overhead by shutting my office and having me and my other employees work out of my home.

❑ Hunted down businesses that had laid off their in-house writers and designers and given aggressive prices for us to take over this work.

❑ Taken on more typesetting work—especially resumes for other displaced employees.

❑ Looked for newsletter training and set up work from clients who were moving newsletters back in-house.

❑ Taken an even more cost-effectiveness stance than I had before—encouraging everyone to cut back on size, use smaller formats and so on.

Realize that when economic times get tough, clients focus on the short term. It's easy for them to ignore a long-term tool like a newsletter. Your job to to take a short-term perspective along with your clients. Help them trim costs right away. Work with them on other projects like direct mailings and flyers until times get better.

But it's usually not the economy

That said, statistics tell us that it's not bad economic times that send clients walking. In 68 percent of the cases, it's inattentiveness (see page 176 of *Working Solo*).

You're going to be spending a lot of time working with your clients. After a while, it's easy to take each other for granted. Make a note to yourself to do something special for your best clients after each job. It's the little things, not the grand gestures that count. Little things you can do for your clients include clipping articles or funny cartoons and sending them with a quick note. The real gesture is that you are thinking of your clients and valuing their business. "Thank" and "you" are the two most important words for selling your services.

Think of something special to do for the holidays. Send custom-made Christmas cards (showcasing your talents) or a Christmas newsletter.

Figure 8-1:
Christmas News
We sent this newsletter out to clients one year. One client saw it beforehand and wanted to send it to his own list. By combining our print runs and charging our client a small fee, our own newsletter ended up costing us nothing.

The Christmas Chronicle

Published by: **EF** COMMUNICATIONS

Christmas 1987

During the eighteenth century, candles on trees were still commonplace. This often provided some Christmas excitement. Although clever holders were designed to hold the candles steady, the trees remained quite a fire hazard. (About 400 candles were considered adequate for a 12-foot tree.) Pails of water and servants holding long wet mops were kept ready in case of emergency.

Luckily, electric lights, which appeared in 1907, have helped alleviated these dangers. Today Americans decorate over 40 million trees each Christmas. ♣

Christmas in October?

The actual date of the birth of Christ has been frequently debated. One theory says that it was sometime in October. Others say it was during the summer.

One thing upon which scholars generally agree is that today's Christmas celebration replaced the traditional celebrations of winter solstice. In many cultures winter solstice had been celebrated to signify the Earth's renewal in spring from its death in winter. This "victory of light over darkness" was also celebrated by the ancient Romans. The Roman Saturnalia festival honored Saturn, god of agriculture. In 600 A.D. there was an active push to convert people to Christianity. Pope Gregory I issued an edict that the traditions of the people be used to help convert them. As a result, the celebration of Christ's birth roughly replaces winter solstice, which fell around December 22.

But some people must still hold to the standard belief that Christ was born in October. For instance, immediately after retailers take down their Halloween decorations, the Christmas displays appear! ♣

Please Post Early for Christmas

As with many inventions, the Christmas card was born out of laziness. The first Christmas card was sent in 1845 by an Englishman, Henry Cole. Cole sent the card to avoid writing Christmas letters. His primary goal was accomplished with one minor setback. The drawing on the card depicted a family drinking wine and created such a stir that Cole never sent Christmas cards again.

A couple of years later W.M. Egley tried the same experiment with a little more success. At about the same time, someone in the United States heard about Cole's card and produced the first American Christmas card.

American Louis Prang began to print seasonal greeting cards in 1875, achieved great success, and by 1880 use had become widespread. The pressure on post offices soon became so intense, the Postmaster issued the now familiar plea, "Please post early for Christmas!" ♣

The Christmas card that that got Henry Cole in trouble.

Talking Turkey

The turkey originated in the southwest, midwestern, and eastern U.S., southern Ontario, and Mexico. America is the only place the turkey has ever been found wild. Because of this, Benjamin Franklin supported the turkey as America's national bird. [Can you imagine President Reagan delivering an address to the nation behind a podium emblazzened with the emblem of a turkey?]

The Aztec Indians domesticated the turkey and took it to Spain in 1519. Soon after that it was taken to England, where it was served as early as 1590. The Jesuits imported the bird to Bourges near the end of the seventeenth century and it soon spread throughout France. At this time it was already becoming a Christmas dish.

❊ ❊ ❊ ❊ ❊ ❊ ❊ ❊ ❊ ❊ ❊

Under the Mistletoe

Mistletoe dates from pre-Christian days. It is a parasitic plant with no roots of its own that grows mainly on apple trees. The Druids believed that mistletoe would protect them from witches, cure illness, and ensure peace and prosperity.

In Norse legend the evil god Loki made an arrow from the poisonous wood of a mistletoe branch and used it to kill Balder, the sun god. The other gods brought Balder back to life and the mistletoe tree vowed to never harm again and to become a symbol of love. Grateful for the return of her son, Balder's mother Frigga now bestows a kiss upon anyone who passes under the mistletoe.

Our custom of kissing under the mistletoe custom is English in origin. Girls who receive a kiss are supposed to remove a berry. When all the berries are gone, the mistletoe loses its power. This is a good incentive to get to your Christmas party early!

Santa Claus – A Business Profile

One of the most vivid manifestations of Christmas is Santa Claus. In addition to his holiday expertise, Santa is also a pretty remarkable businessman. He accomplishes tasks that large corporations such as Coleco and Federal Express struggle with every day.

Santa manages thousands of elves which produce zero-defect products. (Santa wouldn't spoil a child's Christmas with poor quality.) His delivery system is also untouched by modern technology. Using an eight reindeerpower sled, he delivers 100% of his packages overnight — Federal Express can only claim a 98% delivery rate.

It seems only just to include a biography of this accomplished businessman.

St. Nicholas (Santa Claus) was born in the 4th century in Asia Minor. He later became a bishop and stories still abound of his holiness. As a child, Nicholas studied the Bible in lieu of playing games. He fasted except for taking one meal on Wednesdays and another on Fridays. (He definitely wasn't the plump St. Nick we know now, but more on this later...) Because of his remarkable childhood, St. Nicholas is known as the patron saint of children.

When his wealthy parents died, Nicholas decided to secretly dispose of his inheritance. According to legend, Nicholas heard of a nobleman whose three daughters could not marry because there was no money for their dowries. Upon hearing this tale, Nicholas climbed the roof of the nobleman's house for three nights in a row. Each night he dropped a bag of gold down the chimney. The bags landed in the stockings the girls had hung on the mantle to dry.

The legend of St. Nicholas – and the stockings – spread throughout Europe and was brought to the United States by the Dutch. They called him Sinterklaas, but English-speaking settlers changed it to Santa Claus.

Not until the 1800s did our familiar image of Santa Claus appear. Until then, Santa was a tall, dignified man in long robes. In 1822, Clement Moore's poem, "A Visit from St. Nicholas," changed the appearance of St. Nick. The final makeover came in 1866 when the famous cartoonist Thomas Nast drew a plump Santa with red cheeks.

With the health craze of the 80s, you would certainly have an easier time finding a Santa Claus for this year's Christmas party if we held to image of a tall, dignified Santa rather than the plump, rosy one!

"I have this jingling in my ears."

Christmas Customs Around The World

Australia: Christmas falls in mid-summer when the weather is at its hottest. Much of the celebrating goes on outdoors with lunch eaten at the beach – complete with Christmas tree and turkey! Hundreds of thousands gather in the city parks on Christmas Eve to sing carols by candlelight.

Greenland: Families and friends dance, eat, and exchange gifts in festive all-night parties. Special delicacies, such as mattak – whaleskin stuffed with a strip of blubber – are served. Another favorite is kiviak – raw flesh of small auks (diving seabirds) which are buried whole in sealskin for several months until they reach an advanced stage of decomposition. Anyone interested in dining in Greenland?

Mexico: Nine days before Christmas, children begin acting out the Christmas story. The days are called *posadas*, or lodgings, for the inns where Mary and Joseph stopped on their way to Jerusalem. Each night a family gives their home as a *posada*. Processions led by children carrying statues of Mary and Joseph or lighted candles stop at houses only to be turned away until they reach the *posada*. There they kneel, sing, and place the statues on an altar. Afterwards there is a celebration with food, music, dancing, and *piñatas*.

Russia: The religious Christmas festival is being replaced by the Festival of Winter, with Grandfather Frost taking the place of Father Christmas. Some Christmas customs, however, still persist in the Ukraine where a 39-day fast used to precede the Nativity. Everyone would sit and wait for the first star to appear, then sit down to a 12-course meal. After feasting, they would spread hay on the tables and floor to encourage plenty of horse feed during the coming year and then cluck like chickens to encourage the hens to lay eggs.

Sicily: Sicilians fast from sunset on December 23rd to sunset the next day. Afterwards they light a Yule log and begin feasting. Children await the visit of La Befana. Legend has it that La Befana befriended the Three Wise Men, but was too busy cleaning house to go with them to Bethlehem. The next day she realized that she should have gone but it was too late to catch up. La Befana has traveled constantly since that fateful day. She is pictured with a cane in one hand and a bell in the other to announce her arrival. La Befana fills the stockings of children who have been good; her cane is for the naughty ones. [There is a theory that the legend of La Befana has been propagated by people who hate to do housework!]

Average World Temperatures at Christmas

Fairbanks, Alaska, U.S.A. = -9°	Auckland, New Zealand = 63°
South Pole = 6°	Miami, Florida, U.S.A. = 68°
Oslo, Norway = 25°	Christmas Islands = 70° (How did they
Aberdeen, Scotland = 39°	ever get *this* name?)
Jerusalem, Israel = 52°	Sydney, Australia = 75°

Looking Back on 1987

EF Communications has added new people, expanded its offices, and defined where it's going in 1988...

EF Communications was born in June, 1986. Last June marked our first full year of business, and what a year it's been! Several new clients have joined us: Access Data Services, Metropolitan Federal, Pratt Tool Corporation, marketing consultant Don Raymond, C&C Mechanical, A.J. World Travel, Delker Electronics, American Beauty Cosmetics, and the Neurology Clinic. Our original clients – Arnet Corporation, Washington Penn Plastic, and 1st Computer Systems – continue to grow.

We're growing, too. New additions to our staff are La Jean Tietze, editorial assistant, who joined the company in February, and Jeff Runion, layout/designer, who began in October. Also working on your newsletters are freelancers John Landes, Currey Courtney, and Lydia Hutchinson.

By the first of the year we will have moved to larger offices just down the hall from our present location. (For those of you who regularly stop by, this will be a relief!)

EF Communications continues to focus on newsletter production. We started our own publication, *Newsletter News*, which we hope you have found both informative and enjoyable.

In 1988, our hopes are to become further involved in newsletters and to provide you with a "how to produce newsletters" booklet (which will eventually grow into a book). We want to offer you a Christmas newsletter (such as this one) as an alternative to sending Christmas cards and to expand into other newsletter services as well. Our goal is to continue to find ways to make your company publications better.

We have enjoyed working with all of you this year and are looking forward to what lies ahead in 1988!

When the boom is BOOM

We've been over the doom side of economic fluctuations, now it's time for the boom times. Once you fine-tune your marketing, you may find yourself with too much work to handle on your own. It's now time to hire others.

Your first employee will most likely be an office manager who can help you run errands, collect information, screen your calls (and visitors if you're in an office building), open mail and help with simple desktop publishing or editing. Obviously, your first employee needs to be very flexible in tasks and perhaps in hours since you may only need part time help at first.

For design and writing help, you may want to fill in with other subcontractors, perhaps those who are excellent at what they do but less adept at marketing than you are. Lots of good laid-off writers are out there for the taking.

Because your workload may fluctuate drastically during the month, quarter or year, a great way to avoid problems is to team up with other freelancers.

I'm committed to this structure of a business. I found that, after hiring a few employees, I was managing people and not doing the writing and design work that I love. Some people will tell you that you would then just hire a manager. Don't believe it. As long as you stay within your office walls, it's tough to get people not to see you as the true boss.

If you do decide to hire employees, Figure 8-2 shows a sample structure for a newsletter office. Figure 8-3 shows a sample time sheet for tracking the number of hours worked.

Adjusting to your own fluctuations

If you're the type of person who likes to learn new things and has the confidence to take a few risks, once your newsletter service gets going, you may find that it's not the market that changes. It's you.

Perhaps you're looking for new challenges to break you out of the newsletter routine. The next chapter gives you an idea of how a newsletter services can be expanded to take advantage of new technology and your desire to grow.

Figure 8-2:
Sample staff set-up
If you decide to take the employee plunge, here's one way to organize a staff.

Figure 8-3:
(page 114)
Time sheet
Most newsletter service staff are paid hourly. Use this sheet to keep track of time and payroll taxes.

Staff Set-up

❏ Office manager
    job duties:
    receptionist
    gopher
    data entry
    client file organization
    billing
    accounting
    proofreading

❏ Writer/researcher
    job duties:
    researching
    interviewing
    writing
    editing
    proofreading

❏ Desktop publisher
    job duties:
    computer expert
    computer backup
    typesetting & layout given template

❏ Client representative
    job duties:
    sales
    meetings
    oversees work
    trained as writing and desktop publishing backup

Offsite: Consult with professional designers (if you're more writing-oriented) or writers (if your more design-oriented). Designers provide sketches or final artwork for nameplate and page designs. Writers, editors and proofreaders understand news writing style and help assure quality content.

Time Sheet

Name: _____

Address: _____

City/State/Zip: _____

Phone: _____

Social Security #: _____

Day of Week	Morning		Afternoon		Total
	In	Out	In	Out	
Monday					
Tuesday					
Wednesday					
Thursday					
Friday					
Saturday					
Monday					
Tuesday					
Wednesday					
Thursday					
Friday					
Saturday					
Monday					
Tuesday					
Wednesday					
Thursday					
Friday					
Saturday					

Total Hrs.	
Gross Pay:	
Federal Taxes:	
Soc. Security:	
Net Pay:	

Accounting:	
Federal Taxes	
Social Security	
State Unemployment	

9
Sources of future growth

It may seem odd now, but you may arrive at a point in your newsletter business when you're bored with it. It's tough to maintain the level of excitement generated by starting up a company, finding clients and putting procedures into place. You may still get that excitement by working with new clients but that what if it starts to wear off?

Handling burnout

It's not uncommon for people the in the creative field to experience burnout. Ever present deadlines, long hours and brain-taxing work take their toll. The following are some ideas for rejuvenating your creative juices.

Doing the same thing over and over causes a big part of burnout. Combat it by concentrating on expanding your skills in editing, writing, design and your expertise in computers. Treat yourself to a seminar now and then. Give yourself the time to read about new technologies. Think about how they can be used for your clients' newsletters and desktop publishing projects.

Realize how lucky you are to be doing what you're doing. Compare your best day at your old job compared to your worst day now. Hopefully, your worst day now is still better.

Push the edges out

Much of overcoming burnout can be handled by pushing yourself and setting higher standards for the newsletters you create. The best part about newsletters is that you always have another issue to improve upon.

I learned this from an editor of *Time*... but before I tell this story, you need a little background.

First item: the first version of PageMaker came out in 1985 before the availability of hard drives for Macintoshes. To make matters worse, the floppy disk didn't have enough room for PageMaker, the system software, the layout file and the text files. (Sounds a bit like the days before automobiles, huh?) You had to swap disks back and forth to get everything together. PageMaker was also a bit "buggy" (pardon the pun) and would crash the computer from time to time—usually right before a save.

Next item: the fall Comdex (Computer Dealer Exchange) is the largest trade show in the country—swallowing every available convention site in Las Vegas. It's a zoo.

Okay. Here's my story. My first newsletter was an energetic 16-page publication created by swapping PageMaker disks back and forth on my Macintosh. It was created under impossible deadlines for a Comdex show. I worked late hours for several weeks, then traveled to the show. The company I worked for was a small high-tech firm. We had to pack in and set up our own booth, then man it for the duration of the show. The second day there, I was collapsed on the steps in the standing-room-only concession area eating a hot dog.

A man sat down beside me. We started talking and it soon came out that he was a former editor of *Time*. I stared at him in disbelief, weary from my first experience as an editor and asked, "How to you put together a magazine of *Time*'s caliber week after week without becoming a physical wreck?" He paused, smiled at the dark circles under my eyes and said, "You just do the best you can. Then let it go and try to make the next one better."

I figured that if it works for *Time*, it would work for you, too.

Get online

The world of online bulletin boards is booming. Some of the more popular services have special interest groups or forums for desktop publishers and newsletter editors. You can leave questions, tap into their libraries of ideas and participate in live conferences (usually held in the evenings).

Some services have areas to leave samples of your work and have others critique them. (See appendix). After a day of working alone, you'll feel connected to the outside world.

Franchised newsletters

You may feel the sales frustration of finding and completing work, doing a great job and wishing you didn't have to start from scratch for every job. What if you could resell the same final newsletter to another client?

This desire leads some people into what's called the syndicated or franchise newsletter business. For example, after working with a travel agency newsletter you decide to start offering a standard newsletter to agencies nationwide. You approach the National Association of Travel Agents and buy their membership list. You offer the standard newsletter package with a customized nameplate and back page and sell the newsletters for a set price each.

People have successfully done this for many industries including veterinarians, dentists, optometrists, florists, cleaning services, travel agencies, bookstores and more.

Subscription newsletters

You already have the writing, data collection, graphic techniques and publishing down pat. Perhaps you're developing a real expertise in a certain market. You may find the idea of selling subscriptions to the newsletters you create very appealing.

The first thing to realize is that an equal part of the subscription newsletter field is *marketing*. The success of your newsletter depends not only on the quality of the piece you produce but on how well you're able to sell it to subscribers and—most importantly—get renewals.

It's quite expensive to buy the lists and create the direct mail promotions necessary to fill your base of subscribers. Pricing newsletter subscriptions is also an art. Study this market carefully before taking the plunge. Perhaps, one of your clients will go in on the venture with you. Read the two books in listed in the appendix under *books on subscription newsletters*.

Wonders of technology

Much of the growth and excitement in the newsletter field comes from rapidly changing information technology. CD-ROMs are now being installed on "multimedia" computers. Business marketers are making sophisticated use of fax machines and faxes connected to computers to create fax-on-demand systems.

Some newsletters are distributed on disk and contain back issue articles as well. New software allows you to format and upload newsletters to computer bulletin boards. Low-cost color publishing is still in its infancy and will soon be something we're all doing.

It's an exciting time to be involved with publishing. Avoid burnout and expand your skills at the same time by reading computer magazines and going to industry trade shows. Enjoy the exhilaration of staying on the cutting edge.

A final tip for free promotion

A challenging and fun career as a newsletter production professional awaits you. Use the guidelines set in this book to get your business off to a fast start. Then, refine and tailor them to your unique operation as you go along.

If you do start your own newsletter business, one last tip for no-cost promotion of your service is to fill out the coupon in the back of this book. It will get you listed under "newsletter production services" in an upcoming *Newsletter Resources Directory*.

Appendix

Organizations

Intl. Assoc. of Business Communicators
One Hallidie Plaza, Suite 600
San Francisco, CA 94102
(415) 433-3400

Newsletter Publisher's Association
1401 Wilson Blvd., Suite 207
Arlington, VA 22209
(703) 527-2333

Public Relations Society of America
33 Irving Place
New York, NY 10003-2376
(212) 995-2230

Society of Technical Communicators
901 N. Stuart St., Suite 904
Arlington, VA 22203
(703) 522-4114

Toastmasters Intl.
2200 N. Grand Ave.
Santa Ana, CA 92711
(714) 542-6793
This organization is good about listing numbers for local chapters in the telephone book.

Publications

Communications Briefings
P.O. Box 587
Glassboro, NJ 08028
(800) 888-2084

Editor's Forum
P.O. Box 1806
Kansas City, MO 64141
(913) 236-9235

In-House Graphics
United Communications Group
11300 Rockville Pike, Suite 1100
Rockville, MD 20852-3030
(800) 929-4824; (301) 816-8950

Newsletter Design
Newsletter Clearinghouse
44 W. Market St.
Rhinebeck, NY 12572
(914) 876-2081

Newsletter News & Resources
EF Communications
6614 Pernod Ave.
St. Louis, MO 63139-2149
(800) 264-6305

The Page
P.O. Box 14493
Chicago, IL 60614

Publish
Integrated Media, Inc.
P.O. Box 5039
Brentwood, TN 37024
(800) 685-3435

Books on newsletters

Editing Your Newsletter
by Mark Beach
F&W Publications
Cincinnati, OH

Marketing With Newsletters
by Elaine Floyd
EF Communications
6614 Pernod Ave.
St. Louis, MO 63139-2149
(800) 264-6305

Newsletters From the Desktop
by Roger Parker
Ventana Press
P.O. Box 2468
Chapel Hill, NC 27515

Newsletter Editor's Desk Book, 4th Edition
by Marvin Arth & Helen Ashmore
EF Communications
6614 Pernod Ave.
St. Louis, MO 63139-2149
(800) 264-6305
(available Spring '94)

90 Ways to Save Money on Newsletters
by Polly Pattison
5092 Kingscross Rd.
Westminster, CA 92683
(714) 894-8143

The Newsletter Sourcebook
by Mark Beach
F&W Publications
Cincinnati, OH

Quick & Easy Newsletters on a Shoestring Budget
by Elaine Floyd
EF Communications
6614 Pernod Ave.
St. Louis, MO 63139-2149
(800) 264-6305
(available Spring '94)

Books on subscription newsletters

Publishing Newsletters
by Howard Penn Hudson
Charles Scribner & Sons
New York, NY

Success in Newsletter Publishing
by Frederick Goss
Newsletter Publisher's Association
1401 Wilson Blvd., Suite 403
Arlington, VA 22209
(703) 527-2333

Books on desktop publishing

Looking Good in Print
by Roger Parker
Ventana Press
P.O. Box 2468
Chapel Hill, NC 27515

The Gray Book
by Michael Gosney, John Odam & Jim Schmal
Ventana Press
P.O. Box 2468
Chapel Hill, NC 27515

Advertising From the Desktop
by Elaine Floyd & Lee Wilson
Ventana Press
P.O. Box 2468
Chapel Hill, NC 27515

Miscellaneous books

Working Solo
by Terri Lonier
Portico Press
P.O. Box 190
New Paltz, NY 12561-0190
(914) 255-7165

The Tightwad Gazette
by Amy Dacyczyn
Villard Books
New York, NY

Writer's references

The Elements of Style
by William Strunk Jr. and E. B. White
MacMillan Publishing Co., Inc.
New York, NY

Associated Press Stylebook
Christopher French
Addison-Wesley Publishing Co.
Reading, MA

The Writer's Marketplace
Writer's Digest Books
Cincinnati, OH

Newsletter seminars

How to Create Newsletters People Will Read
Padgett-Thomspon
11221 Roe Ave.
Leawood, KS 66211
(800) 255-4141; (913) 451-2900

Newsletter Design
Dynamic Graphics Educational Fndn.
6000 N. Forest Park Dr.
Peoria, IL 61614
(800) 255-8800; (309) 688-8866

Producing, Designing & Writing Newsletters
Newsletter Factory
1640 Powers Ferry Rd., Bldg. 8, #110
Marietta, GA 30067
(404) 955-2002

Writing seminars

Advanced Writing & Interviewing
Thomas Hunter
Effective Communications Group
309 Windsor Terrace
Ridgewood, NJ 07450
(201) 444-3147

Time management seminars

Franklin Day Planners
P.O. Box 25127
Salt Lake City, UT 84125-0127
(800) 767-1776
(801) 977-1776

Pre-printed papers

Queblo Images
1000 Florida Ave.
Hagerstown, MD 21741
(800) 523-9080; (301) 739-4487

PaperDirect
201 Chubb Ave.
Lyndhurst, NJ 07071
(800) 272-7377

Credit reporting service

Dun & Bradstreet
(800) 879-1362

Non-profit market

Chronicle of Philanthropy
1255 23rd St., N.W.
Washington, DC 20037

On-line services

America Online
8619 Westwood Center Dr.
Vienna, VA 22182
(800) 827-6364

CompuServe
P.O. Box 20212
5000 Arlington Centre Blvd.
Columbus, OH 43220
(800) 635-6225

Page layout software

Aldus PageMaker 5.0
Aldus Corp.
411 First Ave. S.
Seattle, WA 98104-2871
(206) 628-2320
Mac, Windows

Express Publisher
Spinnaker Software Corp.
201 Broadway
Cambridge, MA 02139
(800) 826-0706
DOS, Windows

FrameMaker
Frame Technology Corp.
1010 Rincon Circle
San Jose, CA 95131
(800) 843-7263; (408) 433-3311
Mac, Windows

Microsoft Publisher
Microsoft Corp.
One Microsoft Way
Redmond, WA 98052
(800) 426-9400; (206) 882-8080
Windows

PagePlus
Serif Inc.
P.O. Box 803
Nashua, NH 03061
(800) 697-3743; (603) 889-8650
Windows

PFS: Publisher for Windows
Spinnaker Software Corp.
201 Broadway
Cambridge, MA 02139
(800) 826-0706
Windows

Publish It!
Timeworks, Inc.
625 Academy Dr.
Northbrook, IL 60062
(708) 559-1300
Mac, DOS, Windows

Publish It Easy
Timeworks, Inc.
625 Academy Dr.
Northbrook, IL 60062
(708) 559-1300
Mac

QuarkXPress
Quark, Inc.
1800 Grant St.
Denver, CO 80203
(800) 788-7830; (303) 894-8888
Mac, Windows

Ready-Set-Go (formerly DesignStudio)
Manhattan Graphics
250 E. Hartsdale Ave., Ste. 23
Hartsdale, NY 10530
(800) 572-6533
Mac

Ventura Publisher
Ventura Software Inc.
15175 Innovation Dr.
San Diego, CA 92128
(800) 822-8221; (619) 695-7891
DOS, Windows

Word processing software

AmiPro
Lotus Development Corp.
55 Cambridge Parkway
Cambridge, MA 02142
(800) 345-1043
Windows

Microsoft Word
Microsoft Corp.
One Microsoft Way
Redmond, WA 98052
(800) 426-9400; (206) 882-8080
Mac, DOS, Windows

WordPerfect
WordPerfect Corp.
1555 N. Technology Way
Orem, UT 84057
(800) 321-4566; (801) 225-5000
Mac, DOS, Windows

WordStar
WordStar Intl., Inc.
201 Alameda del Prado
Novato, CA 94949
(800) 227-5609; (415) 382-8000
DOS

Photo retouch & illustration software

Adobe Photoshop
Adobe Illustrator
Adobe Systems Inc.
P.O. Box 7900
Mountain View, CA 94039
(800) 833-6687; (415) 961-4400
Mac, Windows

CorelDraw
Corel Systems Corp.
1600 Carling Ave.
Ottawa, Ont., Canada K1Z 8R7
(613) 728-8200
Windows

Calendar making software

CalendarMaker
CE Software, Inc.
P.O. Box 65580
W. Des Moines, IA 50265
(515) 224-1995

Database software

FileMaker
Claris Corp.
Box 58161, MSC 11
Santa Clara, CA 95052
(408) 727-8227
Mac, Windows

Microsoft Excel
Microsoft Corp.
One Microsoft Way
Redmond, WA 98052
(800) 426-9400; (206) 882-8080
Mac, Windows

Clip art

Ad Builder & SCAN
Multi-Ad Services, Inc.
1720 W. Detweiller Dr.
Peoria, IL 61615-1695
(800) 447-1950; (309) 692-1530

Art for the Church
Communication Resources
4150 Belden Village St., 4th Fl.
North Canton, OH 44718
800-992-2144

Artbeats
P.O. Box 1287
Myrtle Creek, OR 97457
(800) 822-0772

Arts & Letters
15926 Midway Rd.
Dallas, TX 75244
(214) 661-8960

ClickArt
T/Maker Co.
1390 Villa St.
Mountain View, CA 94041
415-962-0195

Cliptures
Dream Maker Software
925 W. Kenyon Ave., Ste. 16
Englewood, CO 80110
(800) 876-5665

CorelDraw
Corel Systems Corp.
Corel Bldg.
1600 Carling Ave.
Ottawa, Ont. Canada K1Z 8R7
(613) 728-8200

Designer's Club, Electronic Clipper
Dynamic Graphics, Inc.
6000 N. Forest Park Dr.
P.O. Box 1901
Peoria, IL 61656-1901
(800) 255-8800

Gazelle Technologies, Inc./EduCorp
7434 Trade St.
San Diego, CA 92121
(800) 843-9497; (619) 536-9999

Images with Impact
3G Graphics
114 Second Ave. S., Ste. 104
Edmonds, WA 98020
(800) 456-0234

PFS: Power Album
Spinnaker Software Corp.
201 Broadway
Cambridge, MA 02139
(800) 826-0706

Volk Clip Art
P.O. Box 347
Washington, IL 61571-9982
(800) 227-7048

Clip Photos

CD Stock
3M
3M Center Blvd. 200-9W-07
St. Paul, MN 55144-1000
(800) 447-1858: (612) 722-4895

Comstock Desktop Photography
Comstock, Inc.
30 Irving Pl.
New York, NY 10003
(800) 225-2727; (212) 353-8600

Digital Photographics
Husom & Rose Photographics
1988 Stanford Ave.
St. Paul, MN 55105
(612) 699-1858

Gazelle Technologies, Inc./EduCorp
7434 Trade St.
San Diego, CA 92121
(800) 843-9497; (619) 536-9999

Photo CD
Eastman Kodak Company
343 State St.
Rochester, NY 14650
(800) 242-2424

PhotoDisc, Inc.
2013 4th Ave., Ste. 403
Seattle, WA 98121
(206) 441-9355

PhotoLibrary
ZSoft
P.O. Box 2030
Shingle Springs, CA 95682
(800) 843-5514

Cartoons

Cartoons by Johns
P.O. Box 1300
Pebble Beach, CA 93953
(408) 649-0303

Farcus Cartoons, Inc.
P.O. Box 3006, Station C
Ottawa, Canada K1Y 4J3
(613) 235-5944

Funny Business
Sandhill Arts
P.O. Box 7298
Menlo Park, CA 94026
(800) 854-0717; (415) 854-0717

Computer user groups

PC:
Association of PC User Groups
to locate a user group by zip code or area code call:
(914) 876-6678

Macintosh:
Apple User Group Support
(408) 461-5700

Index

Newsletter Resources Catalog

Marketing With Newsletters, by Elaine Floyd
(EF Communications); 230 pages; $24.95

Every newsletter has promotional goals—from increasing sales or memberships to winning community support. Use the 1000s of ideas listed in this book to win more business or support faster.

You'll learn how to choose content that spurs people into action, develop a newsletter marketing plan, find other people to write it for you, target your best prospects, save money without sacrificing results, and more. Contains over 200 illustrations and sidebars.

Making Money Writing Newsletters, by Elaine Floyd
(EF Communications); 138 pages; $29.95

Turn your newsletter writing and design skills into a lucrative career or sideline. This book shares the secrets you need to find good clients, promote at low-cost or no-cost and fine-tune your operation. It includes over 50 copy-ready forms and a special lay-flat binding.

Editors of all newsletters will find the organizational forms such as copyright agreements, print purchase specifications, proofreading checklists and reporter forms make every newsletter project run smoothly. It's a great time-saving tool for anyone writing, designing or printing a newsletter.

Working Solo, by Terri Lonier
(Portico Press); 400 pages; $14.95

This book is a must-read for anyone thinking about opening or currently operating a small business. It helps you choose the work that's right for you, set up your operation, find financial backing, keep customers and handle money matters. It includes helpful ideas on organizing and managing your time.

Working Solo is the perfect companion guide to *Making Money Writing Newsletters*.

Newsletter News & Resources, edited by Elaine Floyd (EF Communications); 8 pages, six times yearly; $59.95

Includes tips for saving time and money, evaluations of the best desktop publishing software for newsletters, interviews with and ideas from top editors and other in-depth information on newsletter writing, reporting, interviewing, design, layout, printing, distribution and evaluation.

Keep your creative juices flowing and inspiration churning with the help of this bi-monthly publication.

Newsletters From the Desktop, by Roger Parker (Ventana Press); 306 pages; $23.95

You need this book if you're going anywhere near a computer to publish your newsletter. Through over 200 examples, you learn practical ways for creating good-looking newsletters.

The book includes ideas for layouts, typefaces and graphics you can put to use immediately. No need to worry about compatibility—the book's techniques are applicable to all page layout programs.

Editing Your Newsletter, by Mark Beach (F&W Publications); 168 pages; $18.50

Recognized as the standard guide for editing and publishing newsletters, this book covers planning, content, writing, photography, graphics, design, printing, and distribution. It contains 100s of examples of newsletters, many in full color.

The Newsletter Editor's Desk Book, by Marvin Arth & Helen Ashmore (EF Communications); 178 pages; $14.95

Too little time for journalism classes? No problem. This concise review of journalism principles is written for editors of special-audience periodicals. It includes how to gather news, write grammatically correct copy, rewrite, edit, write headlines and handle legal matters.

Advertising From the Desktop, by Elaine Floyd (Ventana Press); 425 pages; $24.95

Desktop design secrets unveiled en masse in this illustration-packed guide. The book includes how to capture attention using tricks taught to designers, motivate people to buy, advertise for free, sell with ads, banners and signs, and design fax-friendly materials.

The book's color section includes 24 full-color pages. A software index details the top 12 PC and Mac layout programs.

COMMUNICATIONS

❼ STEP ORDER FORM

STEP ❶ Ordered by:

Name _____

Company _____

Address _____

City _____ State _____ Zip _____

Daytime Phone # _____

STEP ❷ Ship to:

Name _____

Company _____

Address _____

City _____ State _____ Zip _____

Daytime Phone # _____

STEP ❸

Here's my order:

Qty.	Description	Price	Total Price
	Marketing With Newsletters	$24.95	
	Making Money Writing Newsletters	$29.95	
	Working Solo	$14.95	
	Newsletters From the Desktop	$23.95	
	Editing Your Newsletter	$18.50	
	The Newsletter Editor's Desk Book	$14.95	
	Advertising From the Desktop	$24.95	
	Newsletter News & Resources	$59.95	
	MO res. add 6% tax		
	Shipping ($3 for 1st book; $1 add'l books)		
	Total		

STEP ❹ Method of payment:

☐ Check or money order
(to "EF Communications")

☐ Purchase order enclosed

☐ MasterCard ☐ VISA ☐ AMERICAN EXPRESS

Card # _____

Exp. Date _____

Signature _____

STEP ❺ Fast ways to order:

☎ (800) 264-6305

FAX (314) 647-1609

✉ **EF Communications**
6614 Pernod Ave.
St. Louis, MO 63139-2149

STEP ❻ Rest assured:

All EF Communications
products are 100% guaranteed.
If you're not happy with your
order, simply return it for
credit, exchange or full refund.

STEP ❼ Tell a friend:

Please list the names & addresses of friends who would like to see our catalog.

_____ _____

_____ _____

_____

Thank you for your order.

Newsletter Services Directory Listing Form

Please complete all of the following information for your free listing in the next Newsletter Services Directory. Mail to EF Communications, 6614 Pernod Ave., St. Louis, MO 63139-2149 or send via fax to (314) 647-1609.

Company: _____

Address: _____

City/State/Zip: _____

Phone: _____

FAX: _____

Services Provided:

❏ Consulting   ❏ Research

❏ Writing   ❏ Editing

❏ Proofreading   ❏ Photography

❏ Custom illustrations   ❏ Clip art

❏ Design   ❏ Layout

❏ Printing   ❏ Mailing

❏ Desktop publishing   ❏ Franchise newsletters

❏ Other (specify): _____

Type of computer system used (Mac, PC, etc.): _____

Page layout/word processing software used: _____

Do you specialize in certain markets? (If yes, please specify): _____
_____

Please give a brief background of the principals in the company:
_____
_____

Area you service: ❏ local   ❏ statewide   ❏ national   ❏ international

Year business started: _____

Name of person completing this form: _____

Comments on or suggestions for this book: _____
_____

COMMUNICATIONS

6614 Pernod Ave.
St. Louis, MO 63139-2149